D1063350

WOMEN among WOMEN

Anthropological Perspectives on Female Age Hierarchies

Edited by

Jeanette Dickerson-Putman and
Judith K. Brown

University of Illinois Press

Urbana and Chicago

DISCARDED

UNIVERSITY OF TULSA-McFARLIN LIBRARY

First published in 1994 as a special issue of the
Journal of Cross-Cultural Gerontology 9(2).
© 1994 by Kluwer Academic Publishers B.V.
Chapter 9 © 1998 by the Board of Trustees of the University of Illinois
Manufactured in the United States of America
P   5   4   3   2   1

This book is printed on acid-free paper.

Library of Congress Cataloging-in-Publication Data
Women among women: anthropological perspectives on female age
hierarchies / edited by Jeanette Dickerson-Putman and Judith K. Brown.
p.   cm.
Originally published in 1994 as v. 9, no. 2, of the Journal of cross-
cultural gerontology.
Includes bibliographical references and index.
ISBN 0-252-06683-9 (alk. paper)
1. Women—Social conditions—Cross-cultural studies.
2. Social status—Age factors—Cross cultural studies.
3. Dominance (Psychology)—Cross-cultural studies.
I. Dickerson-Putman, Jeanette.
II. Brown, Judith K.
HQ1161.W62   1998
305.4'07—dc21   97-31988
CIP

HQ1161
W62
1998

To Dorothy Ayers Counts, in friendship and admiration

CONTENTS

NANCY FONER

FOREWORD

This volume on women's age hierarchies is a welcome, and significant, contribution to our understanding of age and gender. The essays make clear, above all, that age and gender hierarchies do not exist in isolation. They are closely connected in a variety of complex ways that have crucial implications for the lives of older and younger women alike.

By now there is a growing literature on the way women's status changes, often for the better, as they grow older. Profound age inequalities divide women in many societies, with older women garnering privileges and powers while younger women, for the moment, lag behind. Less is known about the way these inequalities affect actual relations between older and younger women in the domestic arena as well as in wider community settings.

Coalitions and conflicts—these words suggest the multifaceted nature of relations among women occupying different positions in the age hierarchy. Within the family and household, ties of affection, respect, mutual identification, and interdependence often draw older and younger women together despite the age inequalities between them. In the broader community, too, common interests and concerns frequently provide a basis for cooperation.

Yet, as in any hierarchy, there are also typically suppressed antagonisms and tensions—and the potential for conflict. A perspective on age hierarchy, or inequality, emphasizes that older women's power and prestige depend in good part on young women's subordination. Younger women are frequently bound by cumbersome restrictions and at the mercy of older women's, as well as men's, demands and wishes. Age inequalities mean, too, that older and younger women, in certain contexts and situations, have divergent interests and may be divided by deep cleavages.

Age hierarchies, of course, are not static, and this collection reminds us that social changes can affect the delicate balance of power and privileges between young and older women and thus the very nature of their relationships.

The chapters in this volume show, in wonderful complexity, the way age inequalities play themselves out in relations among women in a broad range of settings. Certainly, they demonstrate the kinds of ethnographic, as well as conceptual, insights we can gain by considering that women have places in both the age and gender hierarchies of their societies—and the critical impact this has for women's alliances as well as conflicts.

INTRODUCTORY OVERVIEW:
WOMEN'S AGE HIERARCHIES

In her classic study of the initiation rites for girls among the Bemba, Richards records the lyrics of a frequently repeated song: "The arm-pit is not higher than the shoulder," which she interprets as follows: "As it is impossible to reverse the arm-pit and the shoulder, so it is impossible for the younger ever to reach higher status than the older" (1956:193). This important lesson for young women among the Bemba appears to hold true universally.

The present volume seeks to correct the relative neglect of this important topic, hierarchies of women based on age. It is a subject strategically located at the inter-section of the anthropology of aging and the anthropology of gender. Borrowing from both subdisciplines, we provide ethnographic data from a variety of societies and suggest some tentative interpretations.

Recent scholarship on gender (Atkinson and Errington 1990; Morgen 1989; Sanday 1990; Sanday and Goodenough 1990; Strathern 1987, 1988) has had a significant influence on this volume, but perhaps foremost is the notion that con-cepts of gender and ideologies of gender are flexible, multifaceted, negotiated, achieved, and situational. Sanday (1990:6–7), for example, states that a number of often competing gender ideologies can coexist in a particular society and can be both negotiated and used to implement economic and political goals. Considerations of social identity are also important. Social identity refers to the ways people are culturally categorized as socially significant (Bledsoe 1990; Kopytoff 1990), an identity based on characteristics of age and gender.

Definitions of the appropriate roles for men and women (gender roles) have been affected by and have exerted an important influence on the economic development process. Most authors agree that development has either bypassed or negatively affected the lives of women, primarily because until recently planners and policymakers did not adequately consider the pre-contact activities of women in drawing up plans for development (Boserup 1990; Charlton 1984; Tinker 1990). It is also important to remember that women of different ages can experience devel-opment in different ways.

Current studies of age and gender also consider the relationship between gen-der and power. Barnes (1990:265) explores the relationship between power and opportunity structure. An opportunity structure consists of legal, economic, and social factors that hinder or help individuals secure economic and political power in their communities. Women's access to and control of power change as modified opportunity structures become available during different stages of the life course.

In tracing the historical development of the anthropology of gender, numerous contemporary feminist authors (di Leonardo 1991; Ginsburg and Tsing 1990;

Sanday 1990) have recommended that gender studies move beyond a model that focuses on the relations of men and women to one that also considers relations among women. As Sandra Morgen notes:

> Some of the important new thinking has come from the various efforts of scholars to deconstruct the meaning of woman/womanhood and to examine women's multiple roles, statuses and positions within the power structures of societies. . . . One of the most important influences of the redirection of feminist theory in general, and feminist anthropology in particular, is the exploration of differences among women (Morgen 1989:9).

We focus on the influence of age on the relationships among women. It is generally agreed that all known cultures divide the individual life course into a series of socially defined stages (Keith 1985). Scholars interested in the anthropology of aging women have explored how women's lives change as they become older and enter the later stages of the life course.

Cross-cultural evidence indicates that increased age brings role discontinuity to women and allows them to become more dominant and powerful. There are numerous ways in which role discontinuity brings improvement to older women's lives (Brown 1982; Brown and Kerns 1985; Counts 1985; Kerns and Brown 1992). First, older women experience fewer restrictions on their behavior and mobility. For example, menopause and the cessation of menstrual customs expand the opportunities of women in some cultures. Second, increased age affords women greater ability to exert authority over kin. Particularly relevant here is a woman's ability to allocate the labor of younger women in both her household and domestic group. Finally, in some cultures, older women have the opportunity to participate in extradomestic roles. For example, some older women take on roles as midwives or have important roles to play in initiation and other specialized rituals. These changes in the lives of older women can form the basis for age stratification among women.

Foner (1984) has noted that age stratification exists in any society when "individuals in a society, on the basis of their location in a particular age stratum, have unequal access to valued social roles and rewards" (1984:xiii). This stratification develops between younger and older women as older women "acquire considerable domestic authority, gain prestige in the family and community and become more active in the public sphere" (Foner 1984:69). This privileged position of older women may, in fact, allow them to exert some control over the lives and opportunities of younger women. These age inequalities play a role in shaping individuals' hopes and aspirations as well as their perceptions of themselves and others.

A BRIEF REVIEW OF THE LITERATURE

Apart from Foner, only a few other anthropologists have concerned themselves with the relationship between older and younger women. One of the earliest studies to deal with the subject was LeVine's (1965) overview of intergenerational tensions inherent in the typical family structure of sub-Sahara Africa. Noting that "the polygynous situation is fraught with potentialities for conflict" (1965:193) between older and younger wives, he also suggests that the mother-in-law/daughter-in-law relationship is not a "point of great strain in African extended families" (1965:195). The younger wife's "separate house, independent occupation and freedom to travel on her own prevent her from being excessively dominated" (1965:195).

In an early overview of relationships among women from an evolutionary perspective, Abernethy (1978:133) concludes that "women in the higher levels of a hierarchy will be found to be more informal and able to dispense with the ceremonial attributes of power", unlike their male counterparts. She takes a positive view of this low-keyed style by women in authority.

Bujra (1979), using a more materialist approach, emphasizes the division of labor by sex and women's roles in domestic labor as major factors determining the relationships among women. She notes that in certain societies, women are "withdrawn from productive labour and restricted to purely domestic activities" (1979:32). Cooperation among women in the performance of household tasks does not necessarily lead to solidarity. This is particularly the case in societies practicing patrilocal residence, in which women, though members of the same domestic group and therefore working together and relating to each other, do not do so by choice. The author is looking at this situation from the point of view of the younger women, since in some societies, potential mothers-in-law do indeed participate in the choice of daughters-in-law. (See, for example, Mernissi 1975.)

Sacks (1992), also taking a materialist view, suggests that among agrarian patriarchal peasantries, brides and mothers-in-law would have an "enormous economically destructive potential" were they not kept from colluding. The co-resident women would present a threat to male power in these societies. The "negative social constructions of women's sexuality" (1992:5) and, by implication, the older women's role in keeping the younger women's sexuality in check are measures utilized to keep women divided.

Political economic processes at the global, national, and local levels can also affect the patterns of relations between older and younger women. On the one hand, the increasing intervention of national government into local arenas and individual lives may bring benefits to categories of people, such as the elderly. On the other hand, the increasing scale of political integration also brings bureaucratic categories on the basis of chronological age, which may obscure individuality and personhood for the elderly. The chronological definition of age associated with the political and economic organization of nation-states and the development of industrial capitalism can promote the marginalization and dependency of the aged (Estes 1979; Halperin 1987). Bureaucratic management can undermine the advantage of seniority in a local setting by introducing new bases of authority, resource control, and prestige and by expanding the horizons of younger people, who become unwilling to await their "natural" progression to the top of the age ladder (Dowd 1983; Foner 1984; Paul 1965).

Foner (1984) provides what is perhaps the fullest consideration of the relationship between older and younger women, which she suggests differs in a number of ways from the relationship between older and younger men. For example, unlike women, older men compete with younger men for spouses in some societies. Foner points out the increasing domestic authority that comes to women with age, comparing the relationship between mothers and adult daughters with that among senior and junior wives and with that of mothers-in-law and daughters-in-law. She concludes that "old women are sometimes active agents in upholding and reinforcing social practices that keep young women subordinate to men" and that "deep strains and cleavages" may divide older and younger women (1984:91). (See also Lamphere 1974.)

Female reproductive strategies among humans serve as a focus for several authors. For example, Irons (1983) suggests that such strategies result in a certain opportunism in women's behavior. "The exact set of social alliances sought by women in any particular society probably reflects the relative importance of female allies versus male allies among that group" (1983:193). According to an analysis of data on the Hadza by Hawkes, O'Connell, and Blurton Jones (1989), the reproductive strategies of women past child-bearing determine their exertion in subsistence activities. The gathering work of women among the Hadza is particularly arduous and enervating. The older Hadza women are reported to work harder in gathering food than younger wives do. These findings are remarkable because they are the exact opposite of the general pattern found in other societies. (See Brown 1982.) The older women increase their progeny in this way, by enabling their younger female kin to devote more time and energy to child-bearing and child-care.

This brief review suggests some of the themes explored in the following articles: that social structure and economic activity shape the interaction of female kin; that the bases and character of the hierarchies among women both change over time and have been affected by the processes of culture change and development; that older women may participate in the suppression of younger women; and that there may be a distinguishable female managerial style if women's authority is traditional, recognized, and unquestioned.

These themes, which have remained largely unexplored in the anthropological literature, are the focus of the studies that follow. They are presented in an order reflecting the degree to which these societies have been impacted by global, national, and local political economic processes: a village in Taiwan, a town in Central Sudan, a rural setting in western Kenya, an Andean peasant community, a horticultural village in Melanesia, and a settled Aboriginal community of former foragers. To add an interspecies perspective, we include a study of the relationship between elder and younger female Japanese macaque monkeys in a provisioned setting. The next chapter is a quantified, cross-cultural study of women's age hierarchies in sixty societies from all over the world. Finally, there is an extensive bibliography of ethnographic sources with full information on the lives of women.

In the first article, Rita Gallin reports on her study of mother-in-law/daughter-in-law relations in a Taiwanese village. She examines generational inequality and explores the changes and consistencies over a thirty-year period. Economic development has made it difficult for some older women to achieve the traditional rewards of age, but in some other instances contemporary conditions have reinforced the traditional hierarchy. Gallin notes that income inequality appears to be a determining factor in shaping these intergenerational relationships.

Susan Kenyon also explores the changes that socioeconomic development have brought to the mother-in-law/daughter-in-law relationship. Her data focus on a town in the Blue Nile Province of Central Sudan. Here there is a 'subsociety', a women's world, which, though interdependent with the larger, male-dominated society, nevertheless provides a variety of institutions in which older women, those past childbearing, can exercise leadership and influence. Although many of the former ways are changing, and will change even more in the future, the traditional importance of age and patrilineal kinship remains.

Maria Cattell's study of the Abaluyia of western Kenya focuses on the relationship between grandmother and granddaughter under conditions of rapid social change. In spite of the traditional emphasis on age hierarchy, the relationship between grandmother and granddaughter was once characterized by a certain informality and some blurring of age distinctions, which facilitated the older woman's educational role. Although modern conditions have somewhat eroded the older woman's privileges and have conspired to distance the generations, the grandmother and granddaughter relationship continues to have importance in the lives of older and younger women.

In the Andean peasant community of 'Utani', two complementary types of hierarchical relationships shape the lives of women. Winifred Mitchell explores each of these in her study of this Aymara village. Within the extended family household, the elder women exercise unquestioned authority and extract labor from the young women and girls. However, there is also a community-wide system of prestige among women, based not on age but on being long-suffering. Mitchell suggests that the complementarity of prestige among female peers and elder authority over female juniors may be how the 'Utani' women structure their adaptation to the harsh realities of peasant life, which have persisted over centuries in this part of the world.

Jeanette Dickerson-Putman examines the ways in which past and contemporary systems of age and gender stratification influence the lives of Bena Bena women in the Eastern Highlands Province of Papua New Guinea. She is particularly interested in the ways in which older women's increased domestic authority, expanded opportunity structures, and control of female life-course rituals affect the lives, choices, and interrelationships of younger women.

Victoria Burbank explores the nature of aggression in female interrelationships in an Australian Aboriginal community. She examines in detail numerous cases of 'disciplinary aggression' between consanguineally related women to understand the Aboriginal meanings given to this practice. Burbank concludes that the nature and quality of this aggression should be viewed not as abuse but as one way in which older women provide nurturance to younger women.

Mary S. McDonald Pavelka summarizes some of the findings of her two-year study of the life-course changes and interrelationships of female Japanese macaque monkeys. She finds that the most important and enduring female relationship for these monkeys is the mother-daughter bond. Pavelka also compares and contrasts the aging experiences of human females and female monkeys.

Using a cross-cultural sample of societies, Judith K. Brown explores the nature of authority in the hierarchical relationships of older and younger female kin. She finds that a society's rules for post-marital residence, its way of reckoning descent, and the extent of women's contribution to its subsistence are related, to a statistically significant extent, to various aspects of older women's authority. Unlike other cross-cultural samples, the world-wide sample of sixty societies used to test the hypotheses consists of societies whose ethnographies provide relatively full information about the lives of women. To make this sample available to other scholars for testing hypotheses regarding women's issues, we provide a bibliography for all the ethnographic sources in the final chapter.

This volume presents descriptive accounts of the relationships of women of different ages in a variety of settings. Examples have been drawn from different geographic areas and from societies that vary not only in complexity but also in their responses to contact with the West. The goal of this volume is to stimulate continuing research on the nature of female age hierarchies and to encourage further exploration of other aspects of the relationships among women. As noted at the outset, anthropological research on various aspects of gender has too long ignored the relationships among women, particularly relationships influenced by age.

REFERENCES

Abernethy, V. 1978 Female Hierarchy: An Evolutionary Perspective. In Female Hierarchies. L. Tiger and H.T. Fowler, eds. Pp. 123–134. Chicago: Beresford Book Service.

Atkinson, J.M. and S. Errington 1990 Power and Difference. Stanford: Stanford University Press.

Barnes, S.T. 1990 Women, Property and Power. In Beyond the Second Sex. P. Sanday and R. Goodenough, eds. Pp. 253–280. Philadelphia: University of Pennsylvania Press.

Bledsoe, C. 1990 School Fees and the Marriage Process for Mende Girls in Sierra Leone. In Beyond the Second Sex. P. Sanday and R. Goodenough, eds. Pp. 281–310. Philadelphia: University of Pennsylvania Press.

Boserup, E. 1990 Economic Change and the Roles of Women. In Women and World Development. I. Tinker, ed. Pp. 14–24. New York: Oxford University Press.

Brown, J.K. 1982 Cross-Cultural Perspectives on Middle-Aged Women. Current Anthropology 23(2): 143–156.

Brown, J.K. and V. Kerns, eds. 1985 In Her Prime: A New View of Middle-Aged Women. South Hadley: Bergin and Garvey.

Bujra, J.M. 1979 Introduction: Female Solidarity and the Sexual Division of Labour. In Women United, Women Divided: Comparative Studies of Ten Contemporary Societies. P. Caplan and J.M. Bujra, eds. Pp. 13–45. Bloomington: Indiana University Press.

Charlton, S.E. 1984 Women in Third World Development. Boulder: Westview Press.

Counts, D. 1985 *Tamparonga:* "The Big Women" of Kaliai (Papua New Guinea). In In Her Prime: A New View of Middle-Aged Women. J.K. Brown and V. Kerns, eds. Pp. 49–64. South Hadley: Bergin and Garvey.

di Leonardo, M., ed. 1991 Gender at the Crossroads of Knowledge. Berkeley: University of California Press.

Dowd, J. 1983 Social Exchange, Class, and Old People. In Growing Old in Different Societies: Cross-Cultural Perspectives. Jay Sokolovsky, ed. Pp. 29–43. Belmont, CA: Wadsworth.

Estes, Carroll L. 1979 The Aging Enterprise. San Francisco: Jossey-Bass.

Foner, N. 1984 Ages in Conflict. New York: Columbia University Press.

Ginsburg, F. and A. Tsing, eds. 1990 Uncertain Terms: Negotiating Gender in American Culture. Boston: Beacon Press.

Halperin, Rhonda E. 1987 Age in Cross-Cultural Perspective: An Evolutionary Approach. In The Elderly as Modern Pioneers. Phil Silverman, ed. Pp. 283–312. Bloomington: Indiana University Press.

Hawkes, K., J.F. O'Connell, and G. Blurton Jones 1989 Hardworking Hadza Grandmothers. In Comparative Socioecology: The Behavioural Ecology of Humans and Other Mammals. Special Publication of the British Ecological Society, No. 8. V. Standen and A. Foley, eds. Pp. 341–366. London: Blackwell Scientific Publications.

Irons, W. 1983 Human Female Reproductive Strategies. In Social Behavior of Female Vertebrates. S.K. Wasser, ed. Pp. 169–213. New York: Academic Press.

Keith, J. 1985 Age in Anthropological Theory. In Handbook of Aging in the Social Sciences. H. Binstock and E. Shanas, eds. Pp. 231–263. New York: Van Nostrand Reinhold.

Kerns, V. and J.K. Brown, eds. 1992 In Her Prime: New Views of Middle-Aged Women. Second edition. Urbana: University of Illinois Press.

Kopytoff, I. 1990 Women's Roles and Existential Identity. In Beyond the Second Sex. P. Sanday and R. Goodenough, eds. Pp. 75–98. Philadelphia: University of Pennsylvania Press.

Lamphere, L. 1974 Strategies, Cooperation, and Conflict among Women in Domestic Groups. In Women, Culture, and Society. M. Rosaldo and L. Lamphere, eds. Pp. 97–112. Stanford: Stanford University Press.

LeVine, R.A. 1965 Intergenerational Tensions and Extended Family Structures in Africa. In Social Structure and the Family: Generation Relations. E. Shanas and G.F. Streib, eds. Pp. 188-204. Englewood Cliffs, NJ: Prentice Hall.

Mernissi, F. 1975 Beyond the Veil: Male-Female Dynamics in a Modern Muslim Society. Cambridge, MA: Schenkman.

Morgen, S. 1989 Gender and Anthropology: Introductory Essay. In Gender and Anthropology: Critical Reviews for Research and Teaching. S. Morgen, ed. Pp. 1–20. Washington, D.C.: American Anthropological Association.

Paul, R.E. 1965 Class and Community in English Commuter Villages. Sociologia Ruralis 5: 2–23.

Richards, A. 1956 Chisungu: A Girls' Initiation Ceremony among the Bemba of Northern Rhodesia. New York: Grove Press.

Sacks, K. 1992 Introduction: New Views of Middle-Aged Women. In In Her Prime: New Views of Middle-Aged Women. Second edition. V. Kerns and J.K. Brown, eds. Pp. 1–6. Urbana: University of Illinois Press.

Sanday, P. 1990 Introduction. In Beyond the Second Sex: New Directions in the Anthropology of Gender. P. Sanday and R. Goodenough, eds. Philadelphia: University of Pennsylvania Press.

Sanday, P. and R. Goodenough, eds. 1990 Beyond the Second Sex: New Directions in the Anthropology of Gender. Philadelphia: University of Pennsylvania Press.

Strathern, M. 1987 Dealing with Inequality: Analyzing Gender Relations in Melanesia and Beyond. Cambridge: Cambridge University Press.

Strathern, M. 1988 The Gender of the Gift: Problems with Women and Problems with Society in Melanesia. Berkeley: University of California Press.

Tinker, I. 1990 The Making of a Field: Advocates, Practitioners and Scholars. In Persistent Inequalities. I. Tinker, ed. Pp. 27–53. New York: Oxford University Press.

WOMEN AMONG WOMEN

RITA S. GALLIN

THE INTERSECTION OF CLASS AND AGE:
MOTHER-IN-LAW/DAUGHTER-IN-LAW RELATIONS
IN RURAL TAIWAN

ABSTRACT. This paper compares relations between mothers-in-law and daughters-in-law at two points of time in a Taiwanese village which has changed over the past 30 years from an economic system based almost entirely on agriculture to one founded predominantly on off-farm employment. Using ethnographic data, it describes how women's intergenerational relations in contemporary Taiwan both refute and support the notion that Chinese women, who are unquestionably treated as inferiors in their younger years, usually are obeyed, respected, and cared for in their later years. The paper discusses the role of income inequality in this difference and argues that development in Taiwan has not only perpetuated old models but also created new forms of generational inequality.

Key Words: intergenerational relations, women, China/Taiwan, development, class

> When we were married we cried because we belonged to another family. We had to cook and to serve others. We used to worry would they like our cooking. If they didn't, your mother-in-law beat you. Now we are worthless. Women today are afraid of their daughters-in-law. They dare not criticize them. If you criticize a daughter-in-law she will run away. Daughters-in-law look at you with ugly faces. (Mrs. Shen, 65-year-old mother-in-law)

> Now I don't have to wash clothes and cook. I have time to play. I have a good daughter-in-law. (Mrs. Li, 52-year-old mother-in-law)

Mrs. Shen speaks to the irreverence of daughters-in-law while Mrs. Li describes her daughter-in-law's piety. These very disparate commentaries on women's intergenerational relations in contemporary Taiwan both refute and support the notion that Taiwanese women, who are unquestionably treated as inferiors in their younger years, usually are obeyed, respected, and cared for in their later years (Harrell 1981: 199; Wolf 1972). The purpose of this paper is to explore the roots of these different behaviors by discussing the relations of mothers-in-law and daughters-in-law in Hsin Hsing, a Taiwanese village that has changed over the past 30 years from an economic system based almost entirely on agriculture to one founded predominantly on off-farm employment.[1]

I begin by describing development in Taiwan and discussing the meaning of old age and intergenerational relations in the traditional Chinese family to establish the context for the material that follows. Then, I compare mother-in-law/daughter-in-law relations in Hsin Hsing during the 1950s and the 1980s. In the final section, I consider why mother-in-law/daughter-in-law relations vary in contemporary Taiwan, and I argue that development in Taiwan has perpetuated old models and created new forms of generational inequality.

DEVELOPMENT IN TAIWAN

When the Nationalist Government retreated to Taiwan in 1949, it found the island to be primarily agricultural with conditions not consistently favorable to development. The strategies it adopted to foster economic growth have been documented in detail elsewhere (Ho 1978; Lin 1973; Pang 1987). Here it need only be emphasized that the government initially strengthened agriculture to provide a base for industrialization, pursued a strategy of import substitution for a brief period during the 1950s, and then in the 1960s adopted a policy of industrialization through export.

This latter policy produced dramatic changes in Taiwan's economic structure. The contribution of agriculture to the net domestic product declined from 36% in 1952 to only 7% in 1986, while that of industry rose from 18% to 47% over the same period. Trade expanded greatly, increasing in value from US$303 million in 1952 to US$64 billion in 1986. The contribution of exports to the volume of trade also rose dramatically, from US$116 million (38%) in 1952 to US$40 billion (63%) in 1986 (Lu 1987: 2).

To achieve this transformation, Taiwan's planners did not depend primarily on direct foreign investment. Rather, they relied on capital mobilization within the domestic private sector and an elaborate system of subcontracting to spearhead the growth of manufactured exports. As a result, Taiwan's industrial development is based on and sustained by vertically integrated and geographically dispersed small-scale businesses.

As early as 1971, for example, 50% of the industrial and commercial establishments and 55% of the manufacturing firms in Taiwan were located in rural areas (Ho 1979).[2] Most such businesses are small-scale operations that produce for domestic and international markets; more than 90% of the island's enterprises each employ fewer than 30 workers (Bello and Rosenfeld 1990: 219) and, in 1987, these small businesses employed almost three-quarters (74.2%) of Taiwan's labor force (Directorate General of Budget, Accounting and Statistics 1988: 116–117).

The predominant form these small enterprises take is the family firm. Indeed, 97% of all businesses owned by Taiwanese are family organized (Greenhalgh 1980: 13). Founded with capital drawn almost exclusively from the informal market market of domestic savings and personal loans, these enterprises are fueled by the unpaid labor of family and the underpaid labor of hired workers. Taiwan's economy, in sum, is sustained by a multitude of small firms that cover the island and that provide income for the majority of the population – a population in which wealth is increasingly becoming unequally distributed (Free China Journal 1988: 3; Hsiao 1987).

THE MEANING OF OLD AGE AND INTERGENERATIONAL
RELATIONS IN THE TRADITIONAL CHINESE FAMILY

In the past, and to a large extent today, the Chinese family was an economic unit of production and the fundamental provider of material and social security for the individual. Traditionally, an authoritarian hierarchy based on generation, age, and gender dominated life within the family. The oldest male had the highest status, and women's status, although it increased with the birth of sons and with age, was lower than that of any man. Great emphasis was placed on respect for age differences, and the desires of the young were subordinated to those of the old, just as the wishes of women were subjugated to those of men.

The roots anchoring this hierarchy were "the mores of filial piety (*xiao*) and veneration of age. Filial piety demanded absolute obedience and complete devotion to the parents, thus establishing generational subordination of the children" (Yang 1959: 89). It obligated children to repay parents for nurturing them and ensured old-age security for the elders. Veneration of age demanded a similar obedience. It required children to honor the strategic knowledge and skills of their elders with deference, respect, and compliance. Both principles served as forms of social control by perpetuating the family and the domination of the young by the old.

This domination is well illustrated by the way in which marriage partners were traditionally selected. Marriage brought a new member into the family, joined two people in order to produce children, and established an alliance between families. The needs of the family therefore took precedence over the desires of the individual in the selection of a mate. Such arranged marriages, though serving the needs and interests of the family, were particularly difficult for women. At the time of marriage, a woman severed formal ties with her natal family and moved as a stranger to live in the home of her husband, where she had to be socialized and integrated into the new household. This task fell to her mother-in-law who often disciplined her stringently and treated her harshly.

The tyranny of the mother-in-law can be explained in several ways:

> in terms of necessity to break the newcomer to the ways of her new home, in terms of a revenge for her own lifelong subjection taken on the part of the older woman against the one adult person over whom she was given much power, or in terms of rivalry for the affection of the son (Baker 1979: 44).

The mother-in-law had also once come as a stranger to her husband's family and the birth of a son had improved her status within it and ensured her security in old age. She had spent years nurturing her relationship with her son and tying him firmly to her (Wolf 1972: 32–41). A young bride was seen as a competitor to her claims on her son. If the bride could not be 'broken', she might deprive a mother of her son's loyalty and support.

Coercion, then, was used by a mother-in-law to subjugate her daughter-in-law. In this, she was helped by her son. He had been taught that the goal of marriage was the continuation of the family, not love or personal satisfaction.

He was expected to side with his mother in the case of conflict and to demand his wife's submission – even by physical force. Given this expectation, as well as the close emotional ties he had with his mother, a son acted as his mother's ally to control his wife. She, deprived of his support, and having few resources with which to bargain for better treatment, obeyed her mother-in-law, showed her respect, and cared for her as she aged.

In sum, filial piety and veneration of age buttressed a status system that defined authority and fostered control of the young by the old. Within this rigid hierarchy, daughters-in-law were subjugated by mothers-in-law to ensure the stability of the family and security in old age. Such stability and security, however, were achieved at the price of the immeasurable repression of daughters-in-law. But daughters-in-law, although accepting their low status as dictated by the way in which family life was traditionally organized, could look to the day when the sons they bore would grow up and bring them daughters-in-law who would defer to them and provide for their comforts.

MOTHER-IN-LAW AND DAUGHTER-IN-LAW RELATIONS IN HSIN HSING VILLAGE

Hsin Hsing is a nucleated village approximately 125 miles southwest of Taipei, Taiwan's capital city, and is located beside a road that runs between two market towns, Lukang and Ch'i-hu. Its people, like most in the area, are Hokkien (Minnan) speakers whose ancestors migrated from Fukien, China, several hundred years ago.

In 1958 the registered population of the village was 609 people in 99 households or economic families.[3] Conjugal families predominated, accounting for 66% of village families (55% of the population). In contrast, only 5% of households (10% of the population) was of the joint type, while the remaining 25% of households (35% of the population) was of the stem form (see Table I).

During the 1950s, when no significant industries or job opportunities existed locally, land was the primary means of production. Almost all families derived their livelihood from two crops of rice, marketable vegetables grown in the third crop, and, in some cases, wages from farm labor. Men worked in the fields while women managed the house and children, worked as an auxiliary farm labor force, and, in their 'spare time', wove fiber hats at home to supplement the family income.

As in most of Taiwan, the structure of marriage in Hsin Hsing during the 1950s was framed by Chinese tradition (see Freedman 1979: 290; B. Gallin 1966: 204–213). Yet, because Hsin Hsing was a village undergoing change, tradition had been modified so that a young woman and man were allowed to have some part in the decision about the desirability of their marriage. A brief meeting was arranged during which the young couple could see each other, and each was then asked for an opinion about the tentatively chosen mate. Given the brevity of the meeting, the young couple could not really evaluate each other, except perhaps by appearance and, if they were at all filial, they were not likely

TABLE I
Population of Hsin Hsing village by Family Type, 1958 and 1989[a]

Family	Period	
	1958	1989
Conjugal		
Number and percent of households	65 (66%)	29 (38%)
Number and percent of persons	337 (55%)	135 (29%)
Average number of persons per household	5.2	4.6
Stem		
Number and percent of households	29 (29%)	38 (50%)
Number and percent of persons	213 (35%)	248 (55%)
Average number of persons per household	7.3	6.5
Joint		
Number and percent of households	5 (5%)	9 (12%)
Number and percent of persons	59 (10%)	72 (16%)
Average number of persons per household	11.8	8.0
Total		
Number of households	99	76
Number of persons	609	455
Average number of persons per household	6.2	5.9

Source: 1958, Household Record Book, Pu Yen Township Public Office; 1989, Field Survey
[a] Although the sources of data contained in the table differ, correlations with other statistical materials confirm the accuracy and comparability of the two data sets.

to reject their parents' choices. Consequently, after this initial meeting, the young couple had no further contact with each other until their marriage.

Upon marriage, a young daughter-in-law was immediately saddled with work under the close supervision and scrutiny of her mother-in-law. She was the family drudge, responding to the daily needs and catering to the idiosyncrasies of all family members. Many daughters-in-law considered their situations intolerable, but it was a rare young woman who dared disobey or show disrespect to her mother-in-law. Divorce was discouraged, opportunities to earn an independent livelihood were essentially nil, and husbands provided little support or comfort (R.S. Gallin 1992). A daughter-in-law, therefore, submitted to the will and whims of her mother-in-law and looked to the time when she could assume the role of wife of the head of the family.

The assumption of this role occurred upon the retirement or death of a mother-in-law or upon family division. Most commonly, it occurred upon division because partition of the family was inevitable as a result of internal conflicts born of economically-based problems and general poverty. Sons thought other family members were not contributing equitably to the group's maintenance while daughters-in-law believed the family's 'wealth' and chores were distributed unjustly. Under such circumstances, the idea of family division was initiated – usually, according to villagers – by a daughter-in-law.

Although a very strong and authoritarian family head or his wife could postpone division for a number of years, continuing friction wearied most parents and they agreed to partition. Usually it took place before the death of the father/head, soon after all the sons of the family were married. In such a division, the parents might join the conjugal family of one of the sons, thus forming a stem family. More frequently, however, the parents themselves formed a separate conjugal family as did each of their sons. In either case, parents remained in their own quarters. If they officially became a conjugal family, the new families formed by their sons fed and cared for them, rotating the duties every ten to fifteen days. The parents received a certain amount of pocket money from each son and, if they needed medical care, it was their sons' responsibility to contribute equally to its cost.

From fear of public criticism, as well as from filial piety, children rarely failed in their obligations to parents. A son who had migrated might sometimes be delinquent in sharing the costs of his parents' care, but more often the problem was his wife's inability, because she lived with him outside the village, to do her share of parent-feeding in the rotation. Under such circumstances, the wives of his brothers often refused to assume the duties of the absent daughter-in-law and the mother-in-law, much to her annoyance, had to cook during her migrant daughter-in-law's part of the rotation.

Nevertheless, an older woman in a conjugal family had few pressing responsibilities. Although with family division she lost the role of imperious mother-in-law directing the activities of her daughters-in-law, she continued to enjoy considerable leisure. Her daughters-in-law performed much of her domestic work, and she was free to enjoy her grandchildren and to visit with other retired women in the village.

In sum, during the 1950s, most villagers were tied to the land and because the elders controlled the principle form of productive property, the farm, they retained control over their children who were dependent on them. Even though marriages were arranged with the 'consent' of the young, a woman came to her husband's home as a submissive, exploitable bride. With the birth of a son, however, she earned a place in her husband's family; and with the arrival of a daughter-in-law, she achieved a position of authority as a mother-in-law. Life improved with the onset of old age for a woman. She became a receiver rather than a provider of care, a supervisor rather than a subordinate (R.S. Gallin 1984).

Given this tradition, one might ask how the villagers responded to Taiwan's transformation from an agricultural state to a newly-industrializing nation. During the 1970s, labor-intensive factories, service shops, retail stores, and construction companies burgeoned in the local area. By 1990, 47 enterprises had been established in the village (see Table II), and Hsin Hsing was a highly stratified community. Farming was mechanized, minimizing the need for either a physically strong or a large labor force. In response to these changes, the proportion of stem and joint families increased (see Table I) and villagers

TABLE II
Enterprises operated by Hsin Hsing villagers 1989–1990

Type of enterprise	Number	Type of enterprise	Number
Factories and workshops		*Sales and services*	
Toys and novelties[b,c]	1	Grocery stores[a]	4
Auto mirrors[b,c]	1	Barber shop[a]	1
Auto oil seals[b,c]	1	Beauty parlor[a]	1
Decorative pillows	1	Motorcycle repair and sales	2
Umbrella frames[b,c]	1	Tailor shop	1
Nylon athletic rope finishing[b]	1	Chinese medicine shop	1
Suitcase construction	1	Pinball parlor[a]	1
Sport shoe tongues[a,b,c]	1	Pesticide shop	1
Metal finishing[b,c]	2	Betel nut vending[a]	3
Custom iron springs[b,c]	1	Taxi service	1
Wire sealing[b]	1	Interior design and decoration[a]	1
Puffed rice candy and cereal	1	Fried chicken vending[a]	1
		Juice vending	1
	13		19
Percent of total	(27.7%)	Percent of total	(40.4%)
Agriculture-related		*Other*	
Itinerant vegetable sales	3	Construction and masonry[c]	1
Rice mill	1	Gambling (numbers games)	4
Grape farms	2		
Pig farm	1		
Duck farm	1		
Vegetable farm	1		
Farm labor brokerage	1		
	10		5
Percent of total	(21.3%)	Percent of total	(10.6%)

Total number 47
Total percent 100.0
[a] With the exception of 3 grocery stores operated by men, these enterprises were operated by women.
[b] The owners of these factories produced for export. With the exception of the man producing toys and novelties, all were subcontractors.
[c] With the exception of 1 metal finisher, the owners of these enterprises hired waged labor.

became part-time agriculturalists and full-time, off-farm workers.[4]

The movement of villagers into the rural industrial sector was not limited to men, however. In 1989–90, the majority (56.8%) of married women in Hsin Hsing worked for remuneration while about one-tenth (11.4%) worked without wages in family businesses (see Table III). Theoretically, the earnings of a married woman were her private money, her *sai-khia* (Hokkien),[5] but in practice a woman's ability to accumulate *sai-khia* was a function of her family's economic position. Women whose families were part of the proletariat and sub-

TABLE III
Primary occupation of married Hsin Hsing villagers by Gender[a] 1989–1990

| Primary occupation | Gender | | | | | |
| | Male | | Female | | Row totals | |
	No.	%	No.	%	No.	%
Wage worker	39	40.6	57	59.4	96	41.9
	(35.8%)		(47.5%)			
Entrepreneur[b]	25	76.5	8	23.5	34	14.8
	(23.8%)		(6.7%)			
Worker in family						
business	5	19.2	21	80.8	26	11.4
	(4.6%)		(17.5%)			
Farmer/marketer	5	100.0	–	–	5	2.2
	(4.6%)					
Farmer	27	71.1	11	28.9	38	16.6
	(24.8%)		(9.2%)			
Soldier	2	100.0	–	–	2	0.9
	(1.8%)					
Housekeeper	–	–	13	100.0	13	5.7
			(10.8%)			
Retiree	5	33.3	10	66.7	15	6.5
	(4.6%)		(8.3%)			
Column totals	109	47.6	120	52.4	229	100.0

Source: Field survey
[a] In addition to married villagers, the figures include 5 widowed men and 21 separated women and widows.
[b] The number of entrepreneurs in Table III and enterprises in Table II do not correspond because several men operated more than one enterprise.

proletariat often worked for wages out of economic necessity, and their wages were contributed directly to the family budget, which was controlled by the male head of the household.[6]

The disposition of any earnings of married women whose families were members of the petty bourgeoisie and bourgeoisie, in contrast, varied. Some women were required to deposit their earnings into the family treasury while others were not. Although a family's economic standing played a role in this difference, it was also a product of age and family type. Young women in stem and joint families were often permitted to keep their earnings to use for their individual conjugal units and for future business ventures or investments. Nevertheless, because it was expected that a woman would 'surrender' her *sai-khia* to her husband when they divided from the large family and became a conjugal unit (Cohen 1976: 210–211), wives usually lost or gave up personal control of their private money upon family partition.

Economic development, then, brought new opportunities for women to earn wages, but this did not necessarily have a substantial effect on patterns of male-female relationships. Some women were able to retain control over their earnings temporarily but were expected to surrender control to their husbands once the husband achieved the status of household head. Male supremacy persisted. Given this persistence of traditional gender hierarchy under conditions of economic change, it is reasonable to ask whether traditional generational hierarchy also persisted. Was the domination of the young by the old maintained? Did older mothers-in-law continue to subjugate their daughters-in-law?

One way to begin to answer these questions is to look at the way in which marriages were arranged in the 1980s. It was seen that in the 1950s parents responded to incipient signs of change by seeking their children's consent to the mates they, the parents, had selected. By the 1980s, parents' monopoly on mate selection had disappeared. They were still involved in the negotiations – the maintenance of family continuity required that they retain some control – but opportunities for jobs in the rural and urban areas had expanded free marriage choice among the young.

Sometimes, young people met at work, liked each other, and asked parents for their consent to marry. Other times, young people were 'shy' and thus depended upon the help of kin or neighbors to find a mate. In such cases, arrangements were made for a chaperoned meeting at the introducer's home, a local restaurant, or some such neutral place. After the meeting, if the young couple were agreeable to each other, they began to date, in the Western sense, and negotiations between the families to arrange the marriage began.

Regardless of how a mate was selected, the mutual affection that developed between a young couple during the pre-marriage dating period was a potential threat to a mother. She had nurtured her son's affection for her, and she expected him to act as her ally in the subjugation of his wife. Her son's affection for his wife, however, meant that the young bride was not as helpless in dealing with her mother-in-law as the older woman had been with hers. The husband-wife bond gave a daughter-in-law a decided emotional advantage in her rivalry with the older woman for her son's affections and loyalties.

Yet, as we saw in the quotes cited at the beginning of this paper, not all daughters-in-law were serious rivals to their mothers-in-law. For example, Mrs. Shen, one of the women cited at the beginning of this paper, was the wife of a farmer, and the old couple lived with their son, daughter-in-law, and five grandchildren. The young couple were factory workers. Mrs. Shen maintained the household and cared for her grandchildren, in addition to working with her husband in the fields. She complained that her daughter-in-law's status was higher than hers, that she was dependent on the younger woman and her son, and that she was 'powerless'.

In contrast, Mrs. Li, the other woman cited, was the wife of a successful entrepreneur. While she worked in her husband's business, as did her daughter-in-law and son, she had been able to lighten her own workload by assigning domestic responsibilities to the younger woman. Mrs. Li also had access to the family treasury, to which her daughter-in-law contributed but over which she had no control. Mrs. Li, in short, exerted authority over her daughter-in-law, who complied with her orders and showed her respect.

These women's contrasting situations represent two poles of a continuum on which countless mother-in-law/daughter-in-law relationships existed in the village in 1989–90. Here I present only a few examples to illustrate the variety in these relationships. While I describe the situations of individual women, their lives are not unique; other older women were embedded in similar circumstances.

Mrs. Shih, for example, lived with her husband, son, daughter-in-law, and four grandchildren. The son operated a small enterprise, which he had established with loans from friends and money he had accumulated on his own from off-farm work. In addition to keeping house and working without pay for her son, Mrs. Shih farmed. She had to work in the fields, she reported, because:

> The young don't like to farm and so we [she and her husband] must do it. My daughter-in-law is busy with her work [the young woman worked in her husband's factory] and so I must do it. Also, we can keep the small profit [from farming], and then we don't have to ask them for money.

Mrs. Shih, in short, was trying to make herself indispensable to her daughter-in-law in exchange for food, clothing, and medical care, that is, her basic needs. She was also trying to achieve a modicum of self-sufficiency so she would not have to depend on her children for money and could gain their respect.

Mrs. Hsieh was also making herself indispensable to her daughter-in-law by managing the household and caring for her two pre-school grandchildren while her daughter-in-law worked in a factory. But, in contrast to Mrs. Shih, she had not chosen the role she occupied. Prior to the birth of her first grandchild, Mrs. Hsieh had been a factory worker, as were her daughter-in-law, son, and husband. When asked why she had retired from work, rather than her daughter-in-law, she replied, "I earned less. My son told me to quit. ... They have the money. If you have money, you have the means to improve your position."

Mrs. Huang represents yet another variant of the experience of old age in the village. She lived together with her two daughters-in-law, two sons, and her husband, who, she asserted, made "only a little money" operating a small grocery store in the village. All three women worked in factories. While her daughters-in-law were also responsible for all the housework, they were permitted to retain their earnings even though she was not. This money was added to the *sai-khia* which they had each brought with them upon their marriages. The two women's *sai-khia* represented a sizeable portion of the seed money for the conjugal units which they and their husbands would eventually establish and which their husbands would head.

Their ability to accumulate and control money had allowed them to negotiate a new relationship with their mother-in-law. While they accepted a double burden – thereby releasing Mrs. Huang from domestic work – they looked to the day when the large family would divide and they might achieve a position of authority. As a result, Mrs. Huang held no illusions about her future. She recognized that support in old age was not automatic in a changing world, and she claimed that, "When I retire, I will use my pension for family living. Now if the family can live together happily, that is enough".

Mrs. Huang was aware of the unpredictability of support because there were twelve mothers-in-law in Hsin Hsing who had no married children living in the village. None of the rewards of old age were available to these women. Most of them worked in the fields and at off-farm jobs in addition to maintaining their households. In a number of cases, remittances to pay for their basic needs were not always forthcoming, and many survived at a subsistence level. Their situations were a stark reminder that old age could be a precarious situation and that the supporting features of filial piety, the 'shoulds' and 'oughts' of *xiao*, could be compromised in a world in which, according to Mrs. Shen, "women do what they will ... and a mother-in-law can't do anything about it".

DISCUSSION AND CONCLUSION

In the preceding pages, I have shown that, as recently as 1989–90, few older Taiwanese women living with their daughters-in-law enjoyed the prerogatives of the traditional mother-in-law role. Many complained that they were powerless, that their daughters-in-law did not listen to their orders, did not treat them very well, and looked down on them. Many also voiced apprehension about their futures. Free-choice marriage had strengthened the conjugal bond; a young woman's ability to earn and control money had nourished her defiance and greater sense of independence. A mother-in-law found her daughter-in-law to be a formidable rival – a rival who represented a serious threat to her old age security.

Not all older women, however, lived in situations fraught with such conflict and uncertainty. A few, like Mrs. Li, continued to hold sway over young women, enjoying a mother-in-law's single privilege – commanding the labor of her daughters-in-law so as to lighten her own workload. Their sons remained their allies, and their daughters-in-law submitted to the older women's authority and showed them outward respect and deference. These women had earned a dominant place in the hierarchy that ordered relations between mother-in-law and daughter-in-law; they had realized a comfortable old age.

How can we explain this difference in intergenerational relations which is becoming prominent in this contemporary Taiwanese village? The answer to this question, I contend, is to be found in the political economy of Taiwan. There, state policies adopted to spur industrial development, resulted in the stagnation of the farm sector, the spread of industry to the rural area, and the commodification of the domestic economy. Without income from the land and with the need for cash, Hsin Hsing villagers turned to the off-farm economy for their livelihood.

In some instances, entry into this economy is accomplished through waged labor. Lacking capital and business acumen, families have been sending members out to join the ranks of the proletariat and sub-proletariat. In other instances, entry is gained by establishing small businesses – with capital generated by either fathers or sons – and family members become part of Taiwan's petty bourgeoisie and bourgeoisie. These different paths have profound implications for the situations in which mothers-in-law find themselves.

The older women in this study who were members of the proletariat or sub-proletariat were among the poorest in the village. Some worked to secure their own futures. Others tried to make themselves indispensable to their daughters-in-law in exchange for material support and outward respect. Still others received material support but found their authority challenged or rejected. And a few, whose children were absent from the village, survived at a subsistence level and relived the drudgery and loneliness of the early years of their marriage.

These women had no control over the resources which are important in contemporary Taiwan. The family land they and their husbands controlled represented a secondary source of income, and their sons had a lessened interest in it as an inheritance. Further, their sons' wives were in a position to make a substantial material contribution to the family's security while the older women were not. These mothers-in-law, in short, were dependent on children in whom the major income power rested, and their daughters-in-law had achieved a new bargaining position from which they could defy the older women's traditional authority.

Older women in this study who were members of the petty bourgeoisie and bourgeoisie, in contrast, were among the most financially secure women in the village. Mrs. Li, for example, was an imperious mother-in-law whose daughter-in-law, in her own words, "worked from morning to midnight". The Li family owned a business, which, as productive property, their son and daughter-in-law would inherit. Given the resources at the command of her mother-in-law, the younger woman submitted to the older woman's authority, was deferent, and looked to the day when she would earn a dominant place in the traditional hierarchy that governed relations between mother-in-law and daughter-in-law.

Not all older women who were members of petty bourgeoisie and bourgeoisie households were as fortunate as Mrs. Li, however. Older women such as Mrs. Shih were not able to provide their sons with capital to establish their businesses. Consequently, they had to strive to make themselves a dependable source of help in order to ensure a measure of security. Like their poorer counterparts, such mothers-in-law had few resources to serve as a base from which to demand obedience from their daughters-in-law.

In sum, development in Taiwan has had uneven effects on intergenerational relations among women. In some instances, it is shifting the balance of power between mothers-in-law and daughters-in-law and significantly altering the ability of older women to realize a comfortable old age. In other instances, it sustains and reinforces the authoritarian hierarchy that traditionally has governed relations in the family and subjugated younger women to older women. The norms of filial piety, which continue to be espoused in Taiwan, are unpredictable under conditions of change. Mothers-in-law with or without the resources important in a capitalist economy are correspondingly able or unable to achieve a secure old age. Development in Taiwan has engendered income inequality and has not only perpetuated old models but also created new forms of generational inequality.

ACKNOWLEDGEMENTS

Research for this paper was carried out in collaboration with Bernard Gallin, whose insights have helped me immeasurably. We acknowledge with thanks the organizations that provided financial assistance over the years and made possible our field trips to Taiwan. Specifically, funding was provided by a Foreign Area Training Fellowship (Ford Foundation), Fulbright-Hays Research Grants, the Asian Studies Center at Michigan State University, the Mid-West Universities Consortium for International Activities, the American Council of Learned Societies, the Social Sciences Research Council, and the Pacific Cultural Foundation. We are also grateful to the Chiang Ching-kuo Foundation for funding (1992–94) to analyze our data and to our graduate assistants, Ross Gardner and Li Chun-hao, for their invaluable help.

NOTES

[1] The research on which this paper is based covers the period from 1957 to 1990. The first field trip, in 1957–58, involved a seventeen-month residence in the village. This was followed by two separate studies, in 1965–66 and 1969–70, of out-migrants from the area. The more recent research in the village spanned two months in 1977, six months in 1979, one month in 1982, and eight months in 1989–90. During these visits, my colleague, Bernard Gallin, and I collected data using both anthropological and sociological techniques, including participant observation, in-depth interviews, surveys, and collection of official statistics contained in family, land, and economic records.

[2] Ho (1979) does not disaggregate the data by area, but our observations suggest that throughout the 1960s industry mainly penetrated towns and rural areas within commuting distance of cities, not the more distant countryside such as the village area studied.

[3] The family takes one of three forms in China: conjugal, stem, or joint. The conjugal family consists of a husband, his wife, and their unmarried children; the joint family adds two or more married sons and their wives and children to this core group. The stem family – a form that lies somewhere between the conjugal and joint types – includes parents, their unmarried offspring, and one married son and his wife and children.

[4] See Gallin and Gallin (1982) for a discussion of the reasons underlying the increase in complex families and R.S. Gallin (1984) on the shift in power between generations of women that accompanied the increase. We suggest in these works that a complex family, i.e., one which included many potential off-farm workers as well as other members who could manage the household and care for the land, had a better chance of achieving economic success than did a family of small size. Nevertheless, the reasons for a family's niche in the class structure were multi-faceted and defy easy generalization.

[5] Cash and jewelry are given to a young woman as part of her dowry, the amount varying on the basis of her natal family's economic condition. In contrast to the other items a woman takes with her to her husband's home at marriage, this cash and jewelry (as well as her clothing) are considered to belong to her and not to the family as a whole. Taiwanese call this 'private money' a woman's *sai-khia*. Any money she may be allowed to retain during her married life is said to become a part of her *sai-khia*.

[6] Members of the proletariat are protected by government labor codes and receive wages determined by contract, while members of the sub-proletariat, not benefitting from government legislation, receive casual rather than protected wages. The village also included members of the petty bourgeoisie and bourgeoisie who each owned the means of production but who were distinguished by the fact that the first did not employ waged labor whereas the second had control over labor power.

REFERENCES

Baker, H.D.R. 1979 Chinese Family and Kinship. London: The Macmillan Press, Ltd.

Bello, W. and S. Rosenfeld 1990 Dragons in Distress: Asia's Economic Miracles in Crisis. San Francisco: The Institute for Food and Development.

Cohen, M.L. 1976 House United, House Divided: The Chinese Family in Taiwan. New York: Columbia University Press.

Directorate General of Budget, Accounting and Statistics 1988 Yearbook of Manpower Statistics, Taiwan Area, Republic of China. Taipei, Taiwan: Executive Yuan.

The Free China Journal 1988 Hard to Slow a Rich Man Down in the ROC. August 11: 3.

Freedman, M. 1979 Ritual Aspects of Chinese Kinship and Marriage. In The Study of Chinese Society: Essays by Maurice Freedman. G.W. Skinner, ed. Pp. 273–295. Stanford: Stanford University Press.

Gallin, B. 1966 Hsin Hsing, Taiwan: A Chinese Village in Change. Berkeley: University of California Press.

Gallin, R.S. 1984 Women, Family and the Political Economy of Taiwan. The Journal of Peasant Studies 12(1): 76–92.

Gallin, R.S. 1992 Wife Abuse in the Context of Development and Change: A Chinese (Taiwanese) Case. In Sanctions & Sanctuary: Cultural Perspectives on the Beating of Wives. D.A. Counts, J.K. Brown, and J.C. Campbell, eds. Pp. 219–227. Boulder: Westview Press.

Gallin, B. and R.S. Gallin 1982 The Chinese Joint Family in Changing Rural Taiwan. In Social Interaction in Chinese Society. S.L. Greenblatt, R.W. Wilson, and A.A. Wilson, eds. Pp. 142–158. New York: Praeger.

Greenhalgh, S. 1980 Microsocial Processes in the Distribution of Income. Paper presented at the Taiwan Political Economy Workshop, East Asia Institute, Columbia University, New York.

Harrell, S. 1981 Growing Old in Taiwan. In Other Ways of Growing Old. P.T. Amoss and S. Harrell, eds. Pp. 193–210. Stanford: Stanford University Press.

Ho, S.P.S. 1978 Economic Development of Taiwan, 1860–1970. New Haven: Yale University Press.

Ho, S.P.S. 1979 Decentralized Industrialization and Rural Development: Evidence from Taiwan. Economic Development and Cultural Change 28(1): 77–96.

Hsiao, W. 1987 Changes in Class Structure and Rewards Distribution in Postwar Taiwan. In Research in Social Stratification and Mobility, Volume 6. R.V. Robinson, ed. Pp. 257–278. Greenwich: JAI Press.

Lin, C.Y. 1973 Industrialization in Taiwan, 1946–1970. New York: Praeger.

Lu, M.J. 1987 Promotion of Constitutional Democracy Government's Goal. The Free China Journal October 5: 2.

Pang, C.K. 1987 The State and Economic Transformation: The Taiwan Case. Unpublished Ph.D. Dissertation, Department of Sociology, Brown University.

Wolf, M. 1972 Women and the Family in Rural Taiwan. Stanford: Stanford University Press.

Yang, C.K. 1959 The Chinese Family in the Communist Revolution. Cambridge: MIT Press.

SUSAN M. KENYON

GENDER AND ALLIANCE IN CENTRAL SUDAN

ABSTRACT: Sudanese women have a stock of mother-in-law/daughter-in-law stories, documenting specific sources of tension inherent in this society where marriages are traditionally arranged and local endogamy is preferred within the patriline. In recent years, however, socio-economic developments within the Sudan have led to changes in both family composition and the range of opportunities available to women, which are mitigating this particular relationship and leading to new alliances between women. Drawing on data from the town of Sennar, Blue Nile Province, this paper looks at some of the factors contributing to these changes, as well as considers the various networks of relationships in which women participate when they move to an urban area.

Key Words: Central Sudan, women, life-stages, age inequality, urban adaptation

Not long after I first moved to Sennar, Central Sudan in 1980[1] I was told the following story, said to have occurred recently in a nearby village:

> A girl had a terrible mother-in-law (*nesiba*)[2] who quarrelled with her all the time, saying "do this, do that". She never answered back but just stayed quiet. Her husband was working in Saudi Arabia and when after two years he came home for a visit, his mother also complained to him about his wife, telling him just to divorce her (*illa talagha*). When she heard this, his wife was so upset that she took some of the arsenic (*sibra*) she used to darken her *henna* cosmetics and added it to her *nesiba*'s coffee. *Nesiba* drank two *finjan*[3] ... and then began to vomit. They rushed her to hospital and had her stomach pumped but it was too late. She died a couple of hours later. The police came to investigate and confiscated the coffee cup, in which they found traces of poison. They informed the son, who immediately divorced his wife. He then went home and strangled her with his own hands for killing his mother. The police did nothing. The husband was quite within his rights to kill his wife for having killed his mother.

While there are various interesting details in this story, it represents a dramatic version of the type of mother-in-law story Sudanese women enjoy exchanging. Sympathy in such stories is usually with the young wife rather than the mother-in-law, even when the narrator is an older woman. It is recognised that a daughter-in-law is often treated unfairly by her husband's family, particularly his mother, and many women, especially when discussing such topics in the warm company of their own families and friends, feel they have shared a similar experience.

When we hear a story such as this, it is difficult not to focus on the inequalities it reveals between men and women in central Sudanese society. This society remains patrilineal and, at least ideologically, patrilocal and patriarchal.[4] Gender segregation is a fundamental principle, and while men are expected to be dominant in their relations with women, women should remain modest and secluded, at least in public or in mixed company. In practice, however, such behavior varies. As the story above shows clearly, inequalities exist between women themselves, as well as in the relative power between women and men. In terms of behavior, some women are obviously more equal than others, and a major determining factor is their social age. A young woman shows respect to an older woman, who in turn is not necessarily deferential to a young man.

In contrast to a typical western reaction to this story, which focuses on male-female dynamics, the interest of Sudanese women would be primarily in the dynamics between women, in this case between a young woman and her mother-in-law. Preoccupation with social segregation in Islamic societies such as the Sudan has till recently blinded outsiders to other principles of hierarchy at work. Gender is obviously only one form of differentiation. Certainly in Central Sudanese society, other ascribed characteristics such as age and kinship are equally important in determining status and roles, both within male or female subsocieties[5] and within society at large. Furthermore, as Sudanese people become increasingly mobile, achieved characteristics, based on rank, education or social class, are also affecting these forms of social hierarchy, particularly in urban areas.

This paper investigates such principles of difference among Sudanese women. The focus is on urban women and consideration is given to how such differentiation affects the organization of the women's world in contemporary Sudanese towns.

RECENT SOCIO-ECONOMIC CHANGE IN CENTRAL SUDAN

Within the last thirty years, the Sudan has experienced many changes: economic (for example Bernal 1988, 1991; Duffield 1981; O'Neill and O'Brien 1988), ecological (Ibrahim 1984; Tubiana and Tubiana 1977; de Waal 1989), political (Beshir 1974; Khalid 1985; Sylvester 1977), social (Bedri 1980; Constantinides 1977; Galal-al-din 1980; Ismail 1982; Mohamed-Salih and Mohamed-Salih 1987) and cultural (Bedri 1987; el-Tayib 1987). Industrial development, although bedevilled by problems, has hastened the process of urbanization (Lobban 1975, 1982; Pons 1980), and women themselves have become active participants in the urbanizing process (Kenyon 1984). In my research in a poor (fourth class) district of Sennar, the seventeenth largest town in the Sudan, where most residents have migrated from surrounding rural areas, I found women felt very positive about urban life. They did so in terms of the advantages it offered to them personally, as well as the opportunities it gave their children: schooling, improved medical facilities, employment, a fuller social life. Few of them complained about missing their families in the village, for they continued to visit regularly. Rather they enjoyed the wide networks of pseudokin they built up in the town, which are free of the constraints of rural life. The fact that they invariably had their own home, or their own share of a home, was regarded as infinitely better than being part of their husband's extended household. Patrilocal extended families continue to exist in towns like Sennar, but are no longer the rule as they are in the village. Patrilineal ties are still important, but especially for a young woman, the ties with her own matrikin, her mother and sisters, occupy more of her time and attention.

Marriage remains the most significant event for men and women, and very few people remain unmarried, but patterns are changing. In the towns, a young man no longer leaves the choice of his bride to his mother, and endogamous preferences are less common. Young urban women expect to exert some choice and may play an active role in arranging their marriage.

Two further, related economic factors are also modifying typical household organization in Sennar. As the economic climate inside the country continues to deteriorate, more and more men are turning outside the Sudan for employment, particularly to the Arab States where remuneration is greatest. Consequently, many urban households are in fact headed by women, although the presence of a son, a brother or other male relative, upholds the patriarchal ideal. In addition, women are becoming more independent, economically, either through need or choice or, most commonly, both. Opportunities outside the home are also diversifying, as women are compelled to find ways of earning an income and show increasing initiative in doing so.

THE LIFE COURSE[6] OF SUDANESE WOMEN

In Sennar there continues to be real separation of male and female which extends into all social arenas. This separation begins at birth, when the customary congratulations for a baby girl (but not a boy) enjoins that she may remain a virgin. Gender segregation remains a factor throughout peoples' lives, though the nature of segregation varies with different life stages, as well as for men and women (as noted elsewhere by Young 1965 and LeVine 1975).

Five stages may be distinguished in a woman's life:

Girlhood (al-bit[7]): Birth to Puberty

Girls and boys may play together as infants but this usually stops around the time of circumcision. In Central Sudan both boys and girls are circumcised, usually between the ages of four and eight. Many girls are still subject to both clitoridectomy and infibulation, a form of operation referred to locally as "pharonic circumcision" in contrast to the less extreme "Sunni" circumcision which is legally acceptable.

Little girls start early to help their mothers and their older sisters (including friends) by caring for younger children, washing clothes, and learning to serve guests, in this way showing the proper behavior of respect. Tasks for young boys on the other hand already have a more public orientation, and include running errands to neighbors or to the local store.

Youth (Fem. Sing. al-shaba): Puberty to Marriage

After their circumcision operation, and particularly as they approach puberty, girls are expected to show restraint and modesty in public, or in situations where they encounter men and older women. They should cover their heads on such occasions and even though there is no real seclusion, their movements outside the home become more restricted and visible. They also assume increasing responsibility for household chores under the eye of their mothers and older female relatives.

Once a girl reaches puberty, marriage options begin to be considered seriously. Even for those who are attending school, various choices are explored, both by the girls themselves, as they seek to impress the young men whom they see at wedding ceremonies or other formal social events, and by their mothers and aunts, who exchange news of eligible men when they meet with their friends.

Bridehood (al-arus): Marriage Through Child-bearing

A fundamental distinction in central Sudanese society remains between the married and the unmarried. In towns like Sennar, girls rarely marry before the age of 16, and young men are usually well into their twenties before they and their family can afford the costs of today's weddings[8]. The ceremony itself is the major ceremonial in Sudanese society and the most important event in the lives of both bride and groom. The days before the marriage are filled with excitement and drama as both bride's and groom's families get ready for the event. The bride is prepared for her marriage by her young married sisters and friends, who also teach her the appropriate, and very arduous *toilette* procedures (Boddy 1989; Kenyon 1991a), dances, posture, and comportment.[9]

The term bride, *al-arus*, however, refers to more than simply the period of the marriage ceremony and is a more elastic concept than the translation implies. To some extent, a woman remains a bride as long as she is bearing children.[10] After the birth of each new child, she will again be greeted as a bride, regardless of her age. Each time, she will be recircumcised (*al-adla*) so that she returns to her husband "as a bride".[11] 'Bridehood' refers to the time when a woman is preoccupied with her sexual relationship, her reproductive functions, and her dependent children. As the 'dirt' of sexuality is cleansed by the elaborate use of powerfully perfumed traditional cosmetics, so those cosmetics in turn serve to define this stage in a highly dramatic and sensuous fashion. Hence the proscription that they should only be used by women who are brides.

This is regarded as a difficult time for a woman, not least because of the pain of childbirth and the constant work that child-raising entails. If a young woman has many small children, a younger, unmarried relative, a sister or niece, may come and help her. This begins the process in which the bride gradually asserts authority over younger women (*al-banat* and *al-shebab*), who will come to include her daughters and in turn, at least traditionally, her daughters-in-law.

A young married woman is expected to be submissive and modest in public, and to turn all her energies to her home, the home of her husband and family. To some extent, such women are seen as responsible for themselves and enjoy a certain independence, being no longer dependent members of their fathers' households. As long as their sexuality is evidently important, however, they must also be seen to control their relationships with the other sex. Their honor, and by extension that of their children's family, is vested in their self-control, so that this then becomes the concern of a wider network of relatives, male and female, who try to ensure that the bride's reputation remains unstained.

In other words, it is women who still fall into the category of bridehood whose behavior should most closely model the ideals of modesty and restraint. Till recently, these ideals were protected primarily by the bride's mother-in-law into whose household she moved at marriage. With changes in the urban extended family, they are now more often the concern of the bride's mother, or other older women on whom she depends.

Bridehood is not always a continuous life stage. Rather it is one which a woman repeatedly re-enters as she gives birth to each new child. As her children begin to grow, she in turn is regarded as entering the next life-stage. Another pregnancy, however, plunges her back into the world of bridehood and the restrictions and dependency that this entails.

Womanhood (al-mara): End of Child-bearing Through Menopause

As a woman's children start maturing and sharing some of her tasks, she is able to enjoy more freedom from the demands of bridehood and, depending on the frequency of her pregnancies, to move in and out of the next life stage, that of womanhood. Increasingly she delegates duties and chores to her daughters and begins to participate more actively in the wider networks of women.

Women who do not have small children, and/or who are approaching menopause, have moved on from bridehood.[12] Now they are fully adult women. They are freed from the demands of child-care and are no longer confined to home for that reason. This is when they shift from ascribed to achieved status. At this stage in their lives, women may wield social power both within the world of women and the wider social world. Now they have some responsibilities towards younger women, both *al-arus* and *al-shaba*, to whom they give help and support in various ways inside and outside the home. They have become decision makers in matters affecting both their domestic groups and the larger social arenas in which they are able to participate. They now have a range of choices about their own lives and those around them, and these will be considered in greater detail below. For some, economic independence is sought in addition to social independence and various opportunities become acceptable which are not available to younger women. Women's authority within their own household and family becomes uppermost and in addition, they often achieve status and leadership within neighborhood and district levels in various capacities. Finally, they are able to travel more freely and participate in a range of overlapping arenas.

Old Age (al-ajuza)

Old people are usually referred to as grandmother (al-haboba) and grandfather (al-jidd). As they move through this stage, both men and women are accorded respect and autonomy, although they are increasingly dependent on their adult children. However, within the women's world, it is their younger sisters, al-marat, women in their thirties, forties and fifties, who to all practical purposes run the show. These are the women who are "in their prime" (after Brown and Kerns 1985).

NEW ALLIANCES IN URBAN SOCIETY

Modern urban living gives women many more opportunities than village life as they establish new, usually informal alliances or networks with their neighbors, with friends, and with special interest groups. While the former are based largely on common age, interest groups tend to be more hierarchically organized, although they also remain generally informal. Older women who have greater experience and are able to move more freely offer a type of support which can loosely be called patronage[13] to younger women who are in the process of disengaging themselves from the status of bridehood or who might still be brides but lack other more traditional forms of support. In this way, they begin to participate in a broad range of economic, social and ritual activities. Further-more, services which were formerly provided within the extended family, in urban areas are increasingly being provided by unrelated women, usually for cash.

Both alliance and patronage are characteristically informal and are often related to the wider complex described as wasta (see also Joseph 1982, 1990), which can best be understood as influence or connections, using whom you know to achieve desired ends. Older women, with greater movement and experience, tend to be more influential and have greater access to resources, human and material, than younger women. They thus are in a position to advise, assist, and protect. Permanent patronage ties are rarely established, although a lasting friendship might grow from it.

In the following discussion, I distinguish different types of alliances to show the range of networks in which urban women are now involved. Many women participate in several networks simultaneously and may be patron in one set of ties and client in another.

Social Alliances

Social obligations and ties between women are vital and create a tightly integrated society, which is largely independent of that of men[14] and which consists of many overlapping circles with varying ranges. Visiting is usually done in the late morning or more commonly in the afternoon, and it is the reciprocity of visiting which creates such tight links.

There are at least three different levels of social visiting:

i.   the informal level, which consists of daily visiting with close friends to chat, gossip, drink tea, give each other *henna* decoration, or take smoke baths together;

ii. the semi-formal level, which is based on reciprocal obligations and includes much bigger networks. These visits are made to offer congratulations for a whole range of events: the arrival of guests, a new car, school successes, returned travellers, recovery from a sickness, any occasion on which caring friends can show that they share the happiness. Older women have the freedom to visit more than younger; on the other hand, younger women tend to show respect to older women by visiting them for such semi-formal occasions;

iii. the formal level: *al-karamat*, (sing. *al-karama*[15]), which are also an expression of formal 'duties'. Informal and semi-formal visiting lays the foundation for these more formal events, which are held for a variety of occasions: births, circumcisions, marriages, deaths, homecomings. In urban districts like al-Gul'a, *karamat* are still sometimes put on by a large extended family. More frequently, a woman calls on her network of neighbours, friends and relatives to help with the preparations. She often delegates the organization of these events (which includes calling helpers and guests, selecting menus, assembling equipment for cooking, allocating tasks and providing instruction to the helpers) to particular women (*al-marat*) who are knowledgeable about such rituals but who are also young enough to be able to put in the hard work needed on such occasions and can command a work force of younger women.

Women who are invited to a *karama* are expected to contribute to the expenses, either with services (by helping), with scarce food items (such as sugar) or with financial help. Such contributions are also referred to as 'duties' (*al-wajiba*) and are the glue which holds reciprocal visiting and women's networks together. Such duties cut across age, although it is usually younger women who contribute services while older women are able to pay in cash or kind.

Women of all ages participate in giving duties, including *al-shebab* though they are doing it for their mother or sister. Women only start building up real credit for themselves after their marriage.

Economic Alliances

Although financial support of a woman and her children is regarded as a male duty, many women in urban Sudan today are working outside the home to earn some income. Services which were formerly provided within the extended family are increasingly being provided in urban areas for cash. I have described this as Sudan's "shadow economy" (Kenyon 1987, 1991a) and suggest that this phenomenon is becoming more diverse as the country's economic problems increase. Often men are unaware of the extent to which women are involved in this type of income-generating activity. Typically, women enter the informal economy by relying on their own, or their friends' *wasta*. Many women in Sennar work informally, simply selling small amounts of vegetables or refreshments (tea, coffee) by the side of the road and begin by helping a friend or relative. Some are more ambitious. A few years ago the Women's Market was set up on the outskirts of the main market when a group of (middle-aged) market women went as a group to the District Commissioner's office and demanded their own premises. They were successful and today, in a cluster of simple corrugated iron sheds, tea shops and petty restaurants cater to predominantly women customers in the market. The original holders have now retired but have handed their 'kiosks' (*al-kushuk*) on to younger women from whom they take rent but to whom they also give advice and encouragement. In recent years, younger women have been driven by need to work in the market. For them, the support and patronage of older women is particularly important.

Other occupations such as the midwife are regarded as more traditional even though most midwives now attend a government training program and are subsequently paid a regular allowance by the government. For the most part, midwives are middle-aged women (*al-marat*) who entered their profession as they were emerging from bridehood and who have older children. They trained with a qualified midwife and in turn take student midwives to train with them, following the students' careers with interest and thus reflecting the way some of the older midwives were themselves taught by a relative. They also show ongoing concern for the families of the women whose babies they deliver, circumcising their daughters when the time comes. Most midwives work in the district where they live and provide the only real community health service to those families. Occasionally midwives *can* also be mobilized as a group. For example, they resent the fact that they are not paid a regular salary, like nurses. In 1982, a group of more experienced midwives in Sennar got together to demand a regular, higher salary from the hospital administration. On that particular occasion, they were unsuccessful because they had failed to realize that they were challenging national, rather than local policy, but they have begun to appreciate the power of cooperative action.

Financial Alliances

The saving scheme known locally as 'The Box', *al-Sandug*, is a type of rotating credit system which is particularly popular among women in urban areas of Sudan (Kenyon 1984, 1991a; Rehfisch 1980). Boxes are run mainly by women who are no longer full-time brides, who are felt to have both the time and experience to operate them successfully, who have a certain level of education (for book-keeping) and of income (in order to cover any losses), and who are trusted by the women who save with them. One woman I worked with in Sennar had been organizing various *sandug* for eleven years, ever since she moved to the town from her village. During this period, she is credited with her family's prosperity. Through her savings, they have been able to set up their own transportation business as well as extend their property considerably. She is particularly admired because she offers financial help to the contributors, drawn largely from her own successful experience. She also organizes her *sandug* in a very personal way, deciding herself, on the basis of need, who should have the savings at what time. These so-called "Ladies of the Box" (*Sittat al-Sandug*) are often influential leaders in the larger community of women.

Educational Alliances

Education of daughters and sons is important to urban women. As education for women becomes more widepread, so more women are entering professions like teaching and medicine, both of which are regarded as respectable by society at large. However, the numbers of women in these positions are still small; they are mainly young and few older women occupy positions of responsibility. Furthermore, the lack of female doctors is a real deterrent to women seeking hospital attention, and many more female faculty are needed in higher education, especially to act as role models and supervisors for female students.

Illiterate women also want to learn to read and write, and are turning in large numbers to adult literacy programs, which are government supported and run for women by women. Teachers of the literacy program, the *Mahwal Umiya*, are paid a nominal salary by the government which is supplemented where possible by the students themselves. Their influence on their adult students often extends beyond literacy, and they are providing technical and marketing skills, as well as strong role models for many poor women who have just moved to the town.

Religious and Ritual Alliances

The influence of Islam on women in Sennar is pervasive. It determines the organization of their day and punctuates their thoughts and words. As a formal religion, however, it provides little organization, leadership, or training for them. Women have a tacitly subordinate role in Islam and receive little guidance about Islam itself.

At the time of my research in Sennar, there was one, very exceptional woman in Sennar, who offered women both leadership and guidance, but always within the conventions of popular Islam. The daughter of Jamil, *Bitt al-Jamil*, can be described as a holy woman (a term she never uses herself), a faith-healer, and a seeress. She herself prefers to say she simply has an Opening or a Gift from God. Her Opening is actually a male spirit, but through him, Bitt al-Jamil regularly (three times a week) helps men and particularly women who come to her for help with a range of problems. She is an extremely devout woman, in her mid fifties when I knew her, married to her first cousin for almost forty years. She has made the pilgrimage to Mecca nine times and for 21 years has regularly entered a trance so that she can communicate with God through a spiritual servant named Bashir, Opening of God. In this state people are able to consult with Bashir about a whole range of social, physical, and psychological problems. Both men and women visit her, but women particularly seek the help and advice Bashir is able to offer.

Holy men are common in the Sudan (Trimingham 1949:129ff), but Bitt al-Jamil is relatively unique. Perhaps this explains why she is so successful; because she provides a real need for religious leadership felt by women in the Sudan.

Leaders of the spirit possession cult known as *zar* also provide a form of spiritual leadership and organization to women in contemporary Sudan. The cult, which is highly complex in organization as well as beliefs, is also dominated by older women, *al-marat*. Young women rarely have positions of importance within the cult, though they might have very strong spiritual powers. Promotion within the cult hierarchy, however, is earned through seven years of apprenticeship with another *zar* leader, including sacrifice during seven Rajabiya[16] seasons. One of the present leaders was promoted when still quite young (in her thirties) on the death of her grandmother, a famous leader from whom she had inherited her powers. However, she had recently been widowed and was thus regarded as no longer a bride. Furthermore, it is said that the *zar* spirits do not like dirt (by which they are implicitly refering to sexual relations). By the time a woman commits herself to the cult, rather than simply consulting it, she is no longer sleeping with her husband. She is divorced or widowed, or her husband has taken another wife.

Middle-aged women dominate both the organization and practice of *zar* performances, but many young women attend, some accompanied by their own small children, others not yet married. If these 'brides' or 'youths' become possessed by the *zar* spirits, it is the older women who look after them, protect them from their spirits, and adopt a very caring and protective attitude towards them.

In *zar*, there is a pattern of female inheritance, in that spirits as well as regalia are frequently passed down through the maternal line. Leadership roles and possession by a particular spirit especially are inherited, often from mother to daughter, but sometimes through the broader matri-kin line (and even occasionally through non-related women). In addition, women also need to maintain their status through their own proven personality and behavior. One woman inherited her box of regalia from her mother, who had been a great leader in *zar*, and she attempted to hold ceremonies on her own. However nobody came. You can't be a leader if no one will follow you, observed one of my neighbors wryly.

CONCLUSION

This paper has tried to indicate the range of activities and the broad networks of alliances that are available to women in contemporary urban Sudan. Women beyond the cultural and physical constraints of sexuality and childbirth participate increasingly in a broader social world, which is organized and controlled largely by them. This is a subsociety or shadow culture which exists partly in opposition to, but always interdependently with, the larger, male-dominated society. Younger women who still have to observe the demands of modesty and are still caring for small children are more restricted, but the assistance and patronage of older women enables them to begin an involvement with a wider world than their home. Furthermore, many of the existing institutions within this women's world: social events, savings boxes, markets, schools, and cults, are also structured hierarchically, with older women in charge of organizing the important positions, and using their influence on behalf of younger friends or 'clients'.[17]

Structurally, this may not differ that much from the more traditional, rural organization of the women's world, which was bounded largely by kinship, and where younger women were often constrained by the reality of patrilocal residence. There too, an older woman organized and controlled the more limited activities and networks of younger women. There she is known as *nesiba*, mother-in-law. Just as she was often felt to abuse her position of authority over her daughters-in-law, so too the modern 'patrons' and 'matrons' who are influential in new social networks and organizations sometimes earn resentment from younger women.

Finally, two of the mother-in-law stories I collected in Sennar were rather different from the rest. In these the sympathy of the narrator and of the audiences was definitely with the mother-in-law. In both stories, *al-nesiba* is described as *miskina*, sad or modest, while the daughters-in-law are educated young women, teachers, who treat their mothers-in-law arrogantly and dis-respectfully. Both reject *nesiba's* help (for example when they are pregnant) and both are described as forcing their husbands, who are very much in love with them, to side with them when they quarrel with his mother. In both stories, the young couple moved away completely from the husband's family because of employment, and listeners are left wondering what evil ploy the young wife used to estrange a young man and his poor mother in this way.

Women in al-Gul'a are not yet ready to accept a reversal of the established hierarchy. Many things are changing in urban life, but age is still shown respect, and carries with it attributes of leadership and control. Kinship, particularly patrilineal kin, continues to be very important, and to exert a dominating influence on a family regardless of distance. On the other hand, education, which is so eagerly sought by young and old, may also be bringing with it a new order of differentiation, one based on rank instead of age. It is as yet too early to see how far education is changing Sudanese society but it seems clear that for at least some middle-aged women, it is perceived as threatening as well as liberating.

ACKNOWLEDGEMENTS

Grateful acknowledgement is made to the many people in the Sudan who helped with my research. This paper owes a great deal to the assistance of Nuresham

Muhammad Ahmed, Miriam Idris, Miriam Omar, Halima Ahmed, the late Soad
al-Khoda, Asia Ibrahim, Zachara Ahmed, Fatima Muhammad, Rabha Muhammad, Najat Abbas, and Zachara Jamil.

NOTES

[1] Research in the Sudan was carried out between 1979 and 1985. I lived for two years in
the fourth class district of al Gul'a, Sennar, in Blue Nile Province. After I moved to
Khartoum in 1982, I continued to make regular visits back there. The observations in this
paper are drawn primarily from al Gul'a in the period 1979–1985. The data were updated
by a short return visit in January 1988.

[2] The term *nesiba* refers to both mother-in-law and sister-in-law. As a term of address it
is rarely used and implies a certain hostility which is regarded as inherent in the
relationship.

[3] This is a small handleless cup used for drinking the strong, sweet coffee enjoyed in the
Sudan.

[4] In practice the ideal pattern is found to varying degree. Many marriages are matrilocal
at first, and the couple moves to the groom's home after the birth of their first child.
Furthermore, the preferred marriage between first parallel cousins (FBD marriage) means
that in some extended households, the bride stays in the same house. Her aunt becomes
her mother-in-law, a situation which is felt to ameliorate the tensions inherent in the
mother-in-law/daughter-in-law relationship.

[5] See Tapper's (1978) description of Shahsevan women of Iran. Elsewhere (Kenyon
1991a) I have described this as a shadow culture.

[6] See Hagestad and Neugarten (1985:35). They emphasize that the life course approach
concentrates on age-related transitions that are *socially created*, *socially recognized*, and
shared. The following stages are generalized from the categories which Sudanese women
themselves gave me, and which ranged from four to seven stages. These discrepancies
are discussed in the text.

[7] Some women divide this into three stages: infancy (*al-tifla*), young girl (*al-binaya*, the
term which may be used for a girl before her circumcision), and *al-bit*, which is an
encompassing term. *Al-binaya* is a diminutive form, applied usually to small girls, while
al-bit (classical, *al-bint*) may be used to distinguish a somewhat older child. However, the
distinction is not always made and an infant girl may be called *al-bit*. Apart from during
her circumcision ceremony, when she is addressed as a bride, *al-arus*, a circumcised girl
is not distinguished terminologically in Sennar.

[8] Brideprice (*al-mahr*) continues to be expected as part of the wedding negotiations and
has increased enormously in recent years, mainly because of the remittances from
overseas to which most families now have access. However, it means that many young
men who stay in Sudan simply cannot afford to get married until much later.

[9] The Teaching (*al-Talima*) of a bride varies in formality, but is held for several nights
shortly before her wedding as her friends (including young married women) gather to
help her rehearse her wedding dances and prepare her for the ensuing ceremony.

[10] Boddy (1989:180), in her study of the village of Hofriyati, in Northern Sudan, appears
to disagree with this. She states that a woman only remains a bride until the end of the
month of Ramadan following her wedding:

> And at the 'id as-Saghir', the 'small feast' marking the end of Ramadan, each woman
> married in the previous calendar round receives guests for the last time as an *'arus*, a
> bride. From now on, she is but a wife.

The difference may be a reflection of the contrasting perceptions of themselves that urban
and rural women have. Certainly no woman I knew in Sennar ever thought of themselves

as 'but a wife'.

[11] Even more specifically, she returns as a virgin. A woman might also be recircumcised just before her husband returns from a prolonged absence (such as when he is working overseas), both to increase his pleasure and to make herself more attractive in both their eyes.

[12] This is approximately the same stage that Boddy (1985:107) notes as transitional for women in Hofriyati. However, it is interesting to note that there "menopause signals the end of her reproductive function". In Sennar, rather, it signals the full onset of 'womanhood' when a woman is able to assert herself fully in the world of women and beyond.

[13] Constantinides (e.g., 1978:198) uses the term patron-client relationship in discussing zaar (sic) networks in Omdurman. Her article is significant here because it also emphasizes the range of alliances simply within one institution (i.e., zar) which are available to women within the urban context.

[14] A husband's and wife's networks rarely overlap very much. Even when attending a wedding together, each will give separately and probably not discuss what the other has done.

[15] Al Karama (pl. karamat), literally means generosity and is the term used for a thanksgiving ceremony or offering made to God on occasions of good fortune. It has no set form, but most commonly a sheep is sacrificed and subsequently a meal is shared. The word also means a miracle.

[16] Rajabiya refers to the Islamic month (Rajab) which the zar cult has made particularly its own. During this time, each separate zar group puts on its own karama to reaffirm its ties with the spirits. For the relationship of zar to formal Islam, see Boddy (1989) and Kenyon (1991a and 1991b)

[17] Client is not a word that Sudanese women themselves would use, generally describing all their friends and contacts as 'sisters' or 'sister's daughters' (depending on the age difference).

REFERENCES

Bedri, B. 1980 Sex Socialization and Conjugal Roles in Omdurman. In Urbanization and Urban Life in the Sudan. V. Pons, ed. Pp. 629–646. Khartoum: Development Studies and Research Centre, University of Khartoum.

Bedri, B. 1987 The Sociology of Food in the Fetiehab Area. In The Sudanese Woman. S.M. Kenyon, ed. Pp. 67–91. London: Ithaca Press.

Beshir, M.O. 1974 Revolution and Nationalism in the Sudan. London: Rex Collings.

Bernal, V. 1988 Losing Ground – Women and Agriculture on Sudan's Irrigated Schemes: Lessons from a Blue Nile Village. In Agriculture, Women and Land: the African Experience. G. Davison, ed. Pp. 131–156. Boulder: Westview Press.

Bernal, V. 1991 Cultivating Workers: Peasants and Capitalism in a Sudanese Village. New York: Columbia University Press.

Boddy, J. 1985 Bucking the Agnatic System: Status and Strategies in Rural Northern Sudan. In In Her Prime: a New View of Middle Aged Women. J.P. Brown and V. Kerns, eds. Pp. 101–116. Massachusetts: Bergin and Garvey Inc.

Boddy, J. 1989 Wombs and Alien Spirits: Women, Men and the Zar cult in Northern Sudan. Madison: University of Wisconsin Press.

Brown, J. and V. Kerns, eds. 1985 In Her Prime: A New View of Middle Aged Women. Massachusetts: Bergin and Garvey Inc.

Constantinides, P. 1977 "Ill at Ease and Sick at Heart": Symbolic Behaviour in a Sudanese Healing Cult. In Symbols and Sentiments: Cross-cultural Studies in Symbolism. I.M. Lewis, ed. Pp. 61–84. London: Academic Press.

Constantinides, P. 1978 Women's Spirit Possession and Urban Adaptation in the Muslim Northern Sudan. In Women United, Women Divided: Cross-cultural Perspectives on Female Solidarity. P. Caplan and J. Bujra, eds. Pp. 185–205. London: Tavistock Press.

Duffield, M. 1981 Maiurno: Capitalism and Rural Life in Sudan. London: Ithaca Press.

Galal-al-Din, M.A. 1980 A Socio-economic Explanation of High Fertility Rates in Greater Khartoum. In Urbanization and Urban Life in the Sudan. V. Pons, ed. Pp. 606–628. Khartoum: Development Studies and Research Centre, University of Khartoum.

Hagestaad, G.O. and B.L. Neugarten 1985 Age and the Life Course. In Handbook of Aging and the Social Sciences, 2nd edition. R.H. Binstock and E. Shanas, eds. Pp. 35–61. New York: Van Nostrand Reinhold Co.

Ibrahim, F.N. 1984 Ecological Imbalance in the Republic of the Sudan, with reference to Desertification in Darfur. Bayreuth: Bayreuther Geowissenschaftliche Arbeiten.

Ismael, E. 1982 Social Environment and Daily Routine of Sudanese Women. Berlin: Dietrich Reimer Verlag.

Joseph, S. 1982 Family as Security and Bondage: A Political Strategy of the Lebanese Urban Working Class. In Towards a Political Economy of Urbanization. H. Safa, ed. Pp. 151–171. Delhi: Oxford University Press.

Joseph, S. 1990 Working the Law: A Lebanese Working-Class Example. In Law and Islam in the Middle East. D.H. Dwyer, ed. Pp. 143–159. New York: Bergin and Garvey.

Kenyon, S.M. 1984 Women and the Urban Process: A Case Study from al Gul'a, Sennar. Khartoum: University of Khartoum Development Studies and Research Centre.

Kenyon, S.M. 1991a Five Women of Sennar: Culture and Change in Central Sudan. Oxford: Clarendon Press.

Kenyon, S.M. 1991b The Story of a Tin Box; Zar in the Sudanese Town of Sennar. In Women's Medicine. I.M. Lewis, A.al-Safi and S. Hurreiz, eds. Pp. 100–117. Edinburgh University Press.

Kenyon, S.M., ed. 1987 The Sudanese Woman. London: Ithaca Press.

Khalid, M. 1985 Nimeiri and the Revolution of Dis-May. London: LPI Ltd.

LeVine, R.A. 1975 Adulthood and Aging in Cross-cultural Perspective. Social Science Research Council: Items 31–32, 4:1–5.

Lobban, R. 1975 Alienation, Urbanization and Social Networks in the Sudan. Journal of Modern African Studies 13 (3): 491–500.

Lobban, R. 1982 Sudanese Class Formation and the Demography of Urban Migration. In Towards a Political Economy of Urbanization. H. Safa, ed. Pp. 67–83. Delhi: Oxford University Press.

Mohamed-Salih, M.A. and M.A. Mohamed-Salih, eds. 1987 Family Life in the Sudan. London: Ithaca Press.

O'Neill, N. and J. O'Brien, eds. 1988 Economy and Class in Sudan. Brookfield: Gower Press.

Pons, V., ed. 1980 Urbanization and Urban Life in the Sudan. Khartoum: Development Studies and Research Centre, University of Khartoum.

Rehfisch, F. 1980 A Rotating Credit Association in the Three Towns. Reproduced with postscript by S. El-Nagar. In Urbanization and Urban Life in the Sudan. V. Pons, ed. Pp. 689–706. Khartoum: University of Khartoum Development Studies and Research Centre.

Sylvester, A. 1977 Sudan Under Nimeiri. London: Bodley Head.

Tapper, N. 1978 The Women's Subsociety among the Shahsevan Nomads of Iran. In Women in the Muslim World. L. Beck and N. Keddie, eds. Pp. 374–398. Cambridge: Harvard University Press.

el-Tayib, D.G. 1987 Women's Dress in the Northern Sudan. In The Sudanese Woman. S.M. Kenyon, ed. Pp 40–66. London: Ithaca Press.

Tubiana, M-J. and J. Tubiana 1977 The Zaghawa from an Ecological Perspective.

Rotterdam: Balkena.
Trimingham, J.S. 1949 Islam in the Sudan. London: Frank Cass and Co.
de Waal, A. 1989 Famine That Kills. Oxford: Clarendon Press.
Young, A. 1965 Initiation Ceremonies. Indianapolis: Bobbs Merrill.

"NOWADAYS IT ISN'T EASY TO ADVISE THE YOUNG": GRANDMOTHERS AND GRANDDAUGHTERS AMONG ABALUYIA OF KENYA

ABSTRACT. Among Abaluyia of Kenya relative age (seniority) structures relationships hierarchically among co-wives, siblings and females of different generations. Ambiguous equality and affectionate informality in grandmother-granddaughter relationships mute the hierarchical implications of their different age and generation statuses. This facilitates grandmothers' educational roles although, as grandmothers say, "Nowadays it isn't easy to advise the young". Increased physical, cognitive and experiential distances between these generations resulted from radical changes in the female lifecourse associated with modernization and delocalization. Nevertheless, reciprocal exchanges continue. Granddaughters are also intermediaries in exchanges between older women and their adult daughters. Some grandmothers are denied the companionship and assistance of granddaughters caught in the middle of mother-in-law/daughter-in-law conflicts. Many grandmothers assume parental responsibilities as they deal with the modern problem of daughters' premarital pregnancies. All in all, these intergenerational relationships reveal both cultural persistence and the effects of social change, and continue to have instrumental and expressive value for both grandmothers and granddaughters.

Key Words: intergenerational relationships, age hierarchy, women, grandmothers, Kenya, Africa, lifecourse

GRANDPARENTHOOD AND AGE HIERARCHY

One way of structuring relationships is by age hierarchies in which seniority is based on chronological age, maturational stage, and/or generational status – though these elements are often confounded (Fortes 1984). Juniors are expected to recognize status and power differentials by behaving toward seniors with respect, deference and obedience. The most explicitly age-structured hierarchies are age-group (age-set) systems, found mostly in subsaharan Africa (Stewart 1977) and predominantly male (but see Kertzer and Madison 1981). In these systems the norm is that powerful seniors instruct and direct obedient, respectful juniors. In real life juniors and seniors often struggle for power (Foner and Kertzer 1978; Gulliver 1963; Spencer 1976). Some observers think that age-group systems do not prevent power struggles but rather channel or redirect conflict (Legesse 1973; Spencer 1965) – a reminder that power is multi-faceted and the exercise of power is complex and changeable over time as experienced in the lives of individuals (Kerns and Brown 1992; Riley 1988; Rossi and Rossi 1990; Udvardy and Cattell 1992).

Until recently grandparenthood was a neglected area of research. A 1976 review of the skimpy literature on grandparents in the United States found their roles to be relatively insignificant for themselves, their grandchildren and their families (Wood and Robertson 1976). A decade later, a volume reflecting new research suggested a rather different picture of American grandparents as engaging in a variety of important family roles (Bengtson and Robertson 1985). Some recent research has focused particularly on grandmothers, especially as surrogate parents (Burton 1992; Minkler and Roe 1993) and, among African Americans, as family matriarchs (Burton 1992) and transmitters of culture such as cultural concepts of womanhood passed down from black grandmothers to their granddaughters (Downs 1992).

In the literature on subsaharan Africa, grandparents are sometimes described as being at the top of family hierarchies: for example, West African Tallensi regard grandparenthood as a person's highest achievement (Fortes 1984), and in two societies in East and West Africa, grandfatherhood is a prerequisite to achieving the socially important status of 'elder' (Sangree 1992). Grandparents are educators of grandchildren, grandmothers are providers of physical care. Grandchildren, in turn, do chores for grandparents and often sleep in their grandparents' houses (e.g., Brown 1935; Cattell 1989a; Cohen 1985; Fortes 1949; Moore 1978). In contemporary Africa, the educational roles of grandparents have diminished (Cattell 1989b) but childminding roles and responsibilities, particularly of grandmothers, have continued and even ex-panded (Apt 1987; Bledsoe and Isiugo-Abanihe 1989; Cronk 1991; Ingstad, Bruun, Sandberg and Tlou 1992; Kilbride 1986, 1990, 1992; Kilbride and Kilbride 1990, 1992; Moller 1990, 1992; Sangree 1986, 1992).

Given the large age and generation differences, one might expect grandchildren to behave as juniors to grandparents, to be deferential in behavior, not discuss certain topics such as sex, perhaps avoid physical contact – espe-cially in societies emphasizing seniority, as is common throughout subsaharan Africa (Robertson 1986; Rosenmayr 1988). While this is sometimes the case, greater seniority does not always bring greater respect to individuals as grandparents than they received (ideally, at least) as parents. Grandparent-grandchild relationships often are exceptions to the usual rules of seniority. In many societies grandparents are warmly affectionate and indulgent with grandchildren (Apple 1956). Their relationships may be relatively free of the strains of relationships in which individuals (brothers or co-wives, for example) may be competing for the same resources (Foner 1984).

Even in cultures with extreme avoidance or respect relationships for certain categories of kin, grandparents and grandchildren may be friendly equals in 'joking relationships', as Radcliffe-Brown (1940, 1949) observed long ago. In many ways, joking relationships reverse the respectful behavior children are expected to show to their parents and the avoidance behavior married adults often show to their parents-in-law. Radcliffe-Brown (1940) suggested that both joking and avoidance behaviors are forms of friendship. Carrying this idea further, Drucker-Brown (1982) argued that joking behavior complements avoidance behavior by allowing the expression of emotions which are sup-pressed in kin bonds governed by an etiquette of respect.

Grandparent-grandchild joking relationships are characterized by informality and intimacy, including verbal abuse, sexual jokes and comments, touching, and metaphoric sex such as addressing each other as 'husband' and 'wife' and being potential marriage partners through the levirate.[1] Warmly affectionate, indulgent and joking grandparent-grandchild relationships have been reported throughout subsaharan Africa.[2] Even where this was the case, however, grandparents in indigenous societies, as authorities in local knowledge, were expected to instruct their grandchildren. Joking relational styles blurred this authority aspect of grandparental roles; at the same time they probably created a positive learning environment. Today the picture is complicated because the knowledge of elders is likely to be less highly valued (Albert and Cattell 1994; Cattell 1989b).

Another aspect of grandparent-grandchild relationships is their structural equivalence. For many Africans, grandchildren are the life force which insures their own immortality: grandchildren (not children) replace individuals as they progress from the human to the spirit world (Mbiti 1969; Sangree 1974); it is in grandchildren (or persons of the grandchild generation) that ancestral spirits are reborn (Blacking 1990). Also, grandparents who are approaching frailty and death and grandchildren, especially adolescents, may share a liminal status on the margins of society (Legesse 1973; Spencer 1990; cf. Turner 1969).

RESEARCH SITES AND METHODS

Data for this paper have been obtained from ethnographic fieldwork over the past decade, beginning in 1982; the research is ongoing. It has been carried out among Abaluyia people in western Kenya, primarily in Samia Location and more recently, in Bunyala Location, just south of Samia; and among Abaluyia in the city of Nairobi.[3] The research extended over two years from November 1983 through November 1985, with shorter visits of 4–6 weeks in 1982, 1987, 1990, 1992 and 1993.

Research methods have included participant observation; informal interviews with people of all ages; structured interviews including questionnaire surveys of old people, primary school children and secondary school students; schoolgirls' written accounts of visits to grandmothers; and biographical narratives of older Abaluyia (for details, see Cattell 1989a). A survey of old people of Samia (age 50 and over) was carried out in 1985 in four sublocations of Samia Location (n = 200 women, 216 men; see Cattell 1989a, 1989b, 1992a for details).

SOCIAL CHANGE AMONG ABALUYIA:
MODERNIZATION AND DELOCALIZATION

In the past century Kenyans have experienced extensive socioeconomic change, often referred to by the ill-defined terms, 'social change' or 'modernization'. A useful concept for examining these changes – especially when considering older people – is delocalization, or the shifting of power from local people and institutions to distant centers such as centralized governments and their bureaucracies, and national and foreign economic powers. The original concept of economic delocalization (Pelto 1973; Poggie and Lynch 1974) has been widened to include the delocalization of family tradition and moral authority, or the loosening of family bonds and the authority of elders (Kilbride and Kilbride 1990, 1992), and the development of delocalized family residential patterns (Weisner 1992).

The Samia (*Abasamia*, in their language) are an Abaluyia subgroup dispersed through the hill country surrounding the northern shores of Lake Victoria in Uganda and Kenya and in the lakeside community of Sio Port, Kenya. Another Abaluyia group, the *Banyala*, are scattered among the hills of the lake's southern reaches in Bunyala District and the small lakeside town of Port Victoria (Figure 1).

A century ago people throughout this area lived in small kin-based groups, governed by their lineage and clan elders. They built their houses of local materials, inside defensive walled villages, as described by the first European to visit them, Joseph Thomson (1885). They were subsistence farmers and herders little affected by the world economy or cultural influences other than contacts resulting from numerous local migrations and local cattle raiders (the reason for the walled villages). They had no currency but only the "special purpose money" (Bohannan 1959) of the hoes made by Samia blacksmiths, livestock and grain, with the value of this money locally determined. Their indigenous religion recognized a high god, Were, and the influence of a variety of spirits in natural objects (such as rocks and trees) and the spirits of dead lineage members *(emisambwa)*. Religious practices were carried out by senior males and by specialists who were often old women: *omundu wemisebe* (spirit medium) and *omulakusi* (diviner). Education was the responsibility of parents and grandparents.

During the 20th century this relatively isolated world changed radically under an onslaught of outside influences and externally motivated social, economic and political development: colonialism and nationhood, urbanization, and the introduction of money, cash cropping, wage labor, and various European ideologies and practices including Christianity and formal or literacy education based on the British system.[4] As new opportunities opened up to young people, power and wealth shifted to a considerable degree from local elders to the young, especially young males (detailed in Cattell 1989a). With young people pursuing education, employment, and city life, families became delocalized, or geographically dispersed into 'multilocal' households which today straddle rural and urban locations and growing wealth and social class differences (Weisner 1992).

Delocalization is apparent in many aspects of life. Today most people in rural Bunyala and Samia are peasant farmers. They still grow much of what they eat but also engage in cash cropping, petty trading, local manufacturing, and other activities which bring them shillings – for today, as people say, "it is a world of money". Unlike the "special purpose money" of local hoes, grain and livestock, this is imported "general purpose money" (Bohannan 1959) whose value is set by market forces in which Samia is peripheral. Today people need money for

Map of Samia and Bunyala Locations
Busia District, Kenya

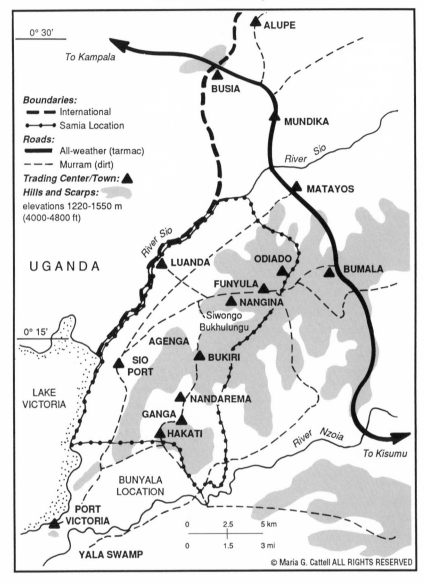

Figure 1.

various necessities, for clothing and school fees, even for food. Many of the
items bought originate outside of Samia and Bunyala, and education is controlled by the national government.

Close to the lake and especially in Port Victoria, fishing is a major industry. In the early 1960s fish were sold or traded in local markets, within a radius of about 45 miles, carried mostly on bicycles (Moody 1963). Today demand from the capital city of Nairobi, several hundred miles distant, dominates, and refrigerator trucks line up on the beaches to buy the catch and transport it to Nairobi.

Nevertheless, in spite of a century of complex and profound change, people living in Samia and Bunyala today are decidedly agrarian or rural in work and lifestyle. It is true that Bunyala and Samia have churches, schools, a hospital, telephone and electric lines, police, government administrators, roads, public transportation. But agricultural work is done with machetes, hoes, and other hand tools. Women still collect and carry (on their heads) water and firewood. All roads are dirt and 'footing it' (by road or footpath) is the most common mode of transportation. Telephone and electric hookups are rare in ordinary homes.

These societies remain strongly kin-based. Clans, patrilineages and extended families are salient in the lives of most Samia and Banyala people, in both rural and urban areas. Individuals (especially younger people) tend to move back and forth between the rural homeland and urban areas. This is especially obvious at Christmas, when many urban dwellers come home for the holidays, and at funerals, which also draw people home. When urbanites come home, temporarily or more permanently at retirement, they come with urban things and ideas, and memories of urban life – but they quickly resume the rural lifestyle in which they grew up.

FEMALE AGE HIERARCHIES:
AMBIGUITIES, CONNECTIONS, CONFLICTS

Hierarchy is pervasive among Abaluyia. Relationships are structured in complex ways in age, gender and kinship hierarchies. Individuals cooperate or compete with each other for power, that is, the ability to influence the activities and behavior of others and to get what they want from others so they are beneficiaries of the flow of "wealth" – goods, money, services and other benefits (Caldwell 1982).[5]

Power over others is exercised in various ways, such as making decisions about work and family life, including what crops to plant, what food to cook, whether to take a sick child to the hospital; and by giving advice, ordering others' daily activities, and sending people to do errands. A person 'on top' expects respect and obedience from those junior. Almost anyone may send a child on an errand: to get something from the house, carry a chair for a visitor, care for a smaller child, go to market, or assist in a variety of domestic and agricultural activities. Heavy social pressure to obey comes from the widespread assumption of obedience by juniors, the numerous examples of it in daily life, and the shame-inducing general disapproval of disobedience. Usually children are quick to obey. The disobedient child may be yelled at, given an unpleasant task to do, or (rarely) beaten. Expectations of obedience are not confined to children: wives should be obedient to husbands, junior wives should follow the lead of the first wife, and so on.

The advantages of higher status individuals are often contested by those they try to dominate, and conflicts in personal relationships are common, though strongly disapproved. The ideal is to have 'peace in the home'. Certain relationships are particularly likely to be conflictual: brothers, fathers and sons, co-wives, and mothers- and daughters-in-law. These relationships often involve struggles for control of valued resources. Males compete for land and sometimes cattle, co-wives for their husband's attention and contributions to their own and their children's maintenance. Mothers- and daughters-in-law struggle for domestic power, personal autonomy, and the attentions of the man (son to one, husband to the other) who created their relationship. Nevertheless, these same relationships can be among the closest of bonds and involve a high degree of cooperation and reciprocity.

In addition, the main factors determining relative status – age or seniority, generational status, gender – are not always congruent, so it is not always clear who is the senior person in a given relationship. There are many ambiguities concerning the proper flow of respect and obedience, command and advice, goods and services. Power may even flipflop over an individual's lifecourse.

The most salient female relationships are among sisters, mother and daughter, mother- and daughter-in-law, co-wives, and grandmothers and granddaughters. Age hierarchy is ever-present.

Siblings always know the order of their birth, and often the order of birth of other sibling groups. If a person asks "Who are your brothers and sisters?" you usually get, without prompting, the names in order of birth. Among siblings, hierarchy is perhaps strongest in childhood, when older siblings order younger to do errands and chores just as adults command children. Later in life, diplomacy becomes important; and sisters may also cooperate to support each other or other females in their families. For example, in one sibling group, when no one was planning to do anything to recognize the college graduation of the thirdborn brother's daughter, the firstborn sister (age about 50) organized her seven younger sisters and brothers for a family celebration. As firstborn, she had the clout and the respect to bring this about in spite of some reluctance from 'below'. While this pleased the graduate immensely, it also emphasized female solidarity in the family and forced family recognition of one young woman's accomplishment.

The mother-daughter relationship is one of mingled respect and affection. It begins with the mother dominant but in time evolves into a relationship of rough equality. Girls are expected to do a great deal of work (much more than boys): childcare, domestic and farming chores. All these are under the mother's supervision. During her childhood, a girl will be disciplined by her mother; mother is the senior, the teacher, the one responsible for her daughter's behavior. But in later life, after a daughter has married and gone to live in another home, often quite far from her mother, their relationship can be more like that of equals. Married daughters are likely to return home for visits, alone or with their children, especially if there are visitors or a funeral when extra help is needed. A daughter may stay for several weeks during which she enjoys working and socializing with her mother. While an adult woman must always respect her mother, she and her mother can get along as friends and co-workers.

The mother-in-law/daughter-in-law relationship is a contrast. A new young wife in her husband's home is under the tutelage of her husband's mother and is junior to every adult in the home; she may even have more than one mother-in-law to answer to if her husband's father has more than one wife (about a third of Samia men are polygynists). Later in life, their roles may reverse; the young bride who was very subordinate may assume the dominant position in her home. If her husband spends most of the year working in an urban area, she may become the de facto manager of the home and farm and the one providing care to her elderly, frail, widowed mother-in-law. If she and her mother-in-law have had a good relationship over the years, the older woman is likely to receive good care from her daughter-in-law, usually with help from grandchildren. But if theirs has been a difficult relationship, the old woman may suffer: her daughter-in-law may be slow in bringing water or may dole out very small portions of food. She may even forbid her children to do errands for their grandmother. Thus the older woman misses out on help with chores, companionship, and the valued social role of grandmother.

In polygynous marriages, the first or 'big' wife ideally manages women's labor for the benefit of an entire homestead. However, tensions and conflicts among co-wives are notorious. There is even a special word for jealousy among co-wives (*esikharikhari*), and stories of 'wicked stepmothers' occur in folk tales and in autobiographical accounts of childhood. A junior wife may resent the senior wife's direction. There may be anger if the husband gives a dress to one wife and not another, or if he pays the school fees of one wife's child and tells another wife that her child can just stay home and help her with work. But cooperation among co-wives is the ideal and also often the reality, especially among women who have been co-wives for a long time. They may act in concert against their husband, quarreling among themselves so there is no peace in the home, refusing to cook their husband's food, and generally making life miserable for him until he gives in to their wishes. Longtime co-wives may unite against a young third wife and try to drive her from the home (Cattell 1992b). They may also support each other as widows (for a case study, see Cattell 1992a).

Thus we can see, even from this brief consideration of female age hierarchies among Abaluyia, that relations of dominance and power connect females in complex ways, entail many ambiguities, and involve both cooperation and solidarity, and competition and conflict. Further, the nature of the power relationship between any two women may shift over the lifecourse and dominance may be reversed.

ABALUYIA GRANDMOTHERS AND GRANDDAUGHTERS

The relationships of Abaluyia grandmothers and granddaughters are characterized – ideally, and often in practice – by informal behavior, affectual warmth and love, friendly teasing, and the grandmother's indulgences. This is in marked contrast to a girl's relationships with adults in the parental generation – except for her *senge*, her father's sister, who is potentially a co-wife and an equal. Out of respect, a girl would not discuss sexual matters with her mother. She not only may discuss sex with her grandmother, but is expected to. Grandmothers should instruct and advise granddaughters concerning sexual and marital behavior, among other things. The advising and learning occur within relationships which simultaneously embrace a friendly equality and the grandmother's authority – as an old woman, a person of high kinship rank, and a person of knowledge.

Grandmother and granddaughter may call each other *mwalikhwa* (co-wife) as a sign of their social equality and a fictitious structural equivalence.[6] Their equivalence may sometimes dissolve into a shared liminality, especially as granddaughters become adolescents and grandmothers become frail.[7] Other ambiguities and uncertainties stem from the changing roles of both grandmothers/older women and granddaughters/girls/young women in contemporary Kenya.

Most older Samia women are grandmothers. Though some girls living in distant urban centers may seldom see their grandmothers, in rural areas (where the majority of Kenyans live) multigenerational households or homesteads are common. In my 1985 survey of Samia old people (age 50 and over), 93% of the women (n=200) said they had at least one grandchild, and most (76%) that they had co-resident grandchildren (Table I: items a,b).[8] Co-resident grandmothers are commonly the father's mother, since a woman moves to her husband's home when she marries. These days, however, growing numbers of children from premarital pregnancies often reside with their mother's mother.

Contact between these generations appears to be high. In many homes I have visited over the past decade I have observed women interacting with grandchildren, often with friendly bantering, teasing, and various expressions of affection. In the 1985 survey, most women (79%) themselves said they saw a grandchild or grandchildren daily; only 10% saw grandchildren as seldom as once a month or only a few times a year (Table I: item c).

Like other family members, granddaughters and grandmothers engage in exchanges of benefits, material and nonmaterial. Their reciprocity forms definite patterns. Grandchildren help with work: 65% of the women surveyed said their grandchildren helped them, while 26% said that their grandchildren were too young to do work (Table I: item e). Grandchildren, in return, were told stories (45% of grandmothers) or given advice (64% of grandmother) (Table I: items f,g). Grandmothers also gave material gifts, especially food. Adult women reminiscing about grandmothers invariably smiled when they recalled the eggs, chickens and dried meat (*omutanda*) their grandmothers gave them.

In 1984, 42 seventh grade schoolgirls wrote essays about visiting a

TABLE I
Samia grandparents and their grandchildren

Characteristic*	Women (N=200)		Men (N=216)	
	N	%	N	%
a) I have at least one GC**	186	93	188	87
b) At least one GC in home	152	76	149	69
c) I see GC				
Daily	157	79	146	68
Once per week	6	3	11	5
Infrequently#	20	10	30	14
d) I see GC often enough	159	80	156	72
e) GC does work for me	130	65	92	43
GC too young to do work	52	26	85	39
f) I tell my GC stories	89	45	65	30
g) I give my GC advice	128	64	114	53
h) GC follow(s) my advice				
Usually	55	43	46	40
Sometimes	57	45	54	47
Never	4	--	4	--
I don't know	12	9	10	9
	128		114	
i) GP** and GC were closer in the old days				
Agree	167	94	190	95
Disagree	10	6	11	6
	177		201	
j) GC sleeps in my house	44	55	21	25
(Subsample: N=80 women, 83 men)				
k) I have at least one dependent GC (women and men combined, subsample, N=252):	74	29%		

Notes
* Categories with few cases are omitted; missing values are not noted. Proportions are based on total N (200 women, 216 men) except as indicated by other totals. Percentages are rounded.
** GC = grandchild/grandchildren; GP = grandparent(s).
\# From once or twice a month to a few times a year.
Source: Survey of Old People of Samia (in Cattell 1989a)
© Maria G. Cattell ALL RIGHTS RESERVED.

grandparent – their mother's mother in all but two cases (the exceptions being mother's fathers). The girls wrote with love and remembered pleasure about planning the trip, the gifts they took, what they did while in grandmother's home, the gifts grandmother gave them when they left. Whether the idea for the visit came from the girl or her mother, the mothers took advantage of the visits to send things to their mothers (the grandmother): food, household items, a blanket, soap, clothes, cigarettes. Half the girls stayed for one to two weeks, a quarter for three weeks or longer. The girls did a variety of chores, and their grandmothers told stories, talked about the way things were done in the past, and gave their granddaughters advice. The advice concerned primarily respecting, obeying and being kind to elders and working hard in school and at home.[9] Each girl went home with a gift from her grandmother; many went with a hen and/or eggs, customary grandmotherly gifts.

In a typical account, Susan Ochieno wrote: "It was on a Friday evening when my mother asked me to go and visit my grandmother who is too old and she is unable to help herself. So on Saturday morning my mother gave me two kilos of sugar, two loaves of bread, one packet of tea leaves, three packets of milk and two kilos of meat. She packed them well in a basket and I started my journey". Susan then described the warm welcome she received and the work she did for her grandmother: sweeping, cooking, fetching wood and water, washing dishes. On Sunday, Susan was ready to return to her parents' home. "She [grandmother] gave me her biggest hen. She thanked me for helping her and she gave me six boiled eggs and some milk in a gourd. I was very happy and I wished I could visit grandmother again".

People say that a woman loves her daughter's children better than the children of her sons – a statement which probably reflects the close and enduring bonds of many mothers and daughters. Another factor may be that the mother's mother sees her married daughter's children as visitors. Visiting grandchildren may be more attentive than co-resident grandchildren, since the visitor has come specifically to visit the grandmother. Certainly grandchildren see the mother's mother in particular as the giver of nice things and a source of love and happiness.

While these examples create the impression of frequent contact and satisfying exchanges between grandmothers and granddaughters, nevertheless they differ radically from the situation of perhaps only 30 or 40 years ago. In the modern context – within the lifetimes of today's grandmothers – many conditions which promoted closeness and frequent contact have changed. The delocalization of valued knowledge, moral authority, family residence and other aspects of life has increased the physical, experiential and cognitive distances between grandmothers and granddaughters.

Even though 80% of grandmothers in the survey said they saw their grandchildren often enough, 94% said that grandparents and grandchildren were closer "in the old days" (Table I: items d, i). They are surely correct in their assessment, in spite of the human tendency to idealize the past and the continued high frequency of grandmother-granddaughter co-residency. For most of the day, granddaughters of school age are physically separated from grandmothers. Some girls go to nursery school at age 4 or 5, and most get at least eight years of primary education. Many leave home before sunrise (which is at 7 a.m. year round) for the long walk to school; they may not return home till 5 or 6 in the evening. Most secondary schools are boarding schools. Girls lucky enough to get a place in secondary school (not true of the majority of girls) live away from home for nine months of the year. They are co-resident with grandmothers for only three months in a year.

Though many grandmothers urge granddaughters to do well in school and may even contribute to a girl's school fees, school learning and foreign ideologies compete with elders' knowledge (Cattell 1989b; cf. Wanjala 1985). When girls come home from school, at the end of a day or a three-month period, they come with knowledge gained from educated young people, their school teachers, who have partially replaced grandmothers and other elders as possessors of important knowledge.

In the past, most girls slept in *esibinje*, the grandmother's house, until they married. This was a relaxed context in which grandmothers transmitted knowledge and advised granddaughters about sexual and marital behavior and other matters.[10] In my 1985 survey, 275 older Samia women and men said they had known one or more grandparents (the others as children had had no living grandparent), and 80% of them reported having slept in *esibinje* with a grandmother.[11] In a subsample of these elders (n=80 women, 83 men), 55% of the women and 25% of the men said they themselves had at least one grandchild sleeping with them (Table I: item j). However, these are likely to be young grandchildren. Adolescent unmarried girls nowadays are likely to sleep in their mother's kitchen, usually a separate building in Abaluyia homesteads; adolescent boys get their own houses.

As a consequence of these and other changes, including powerful influences of the state and workplace (cf. Mayer and Muller 1986; Plath 1983) and their interactions with the cumulative choices of individuals (Thompson 1981), granddaughters' life experiences differ in many ways from those of grandmothers. Older women's experiences of the modern world, of the world beyond their home area, have been limited. Few grandmothers have ever been formally employed or visited a major city; most do not speak English, the language of schools and modern communication. Now, however, in the 1980s and 1990s, schooling and urban employment, once largely confined to men, are more open to Kenyan women, and growing numbers attend school and spend major portions of their lives in urban areas. Women are marrying later, often after having become mothers as adolescent schoolgirls; some refuse to marry.

One way to examine these differences is to look at changes in female lifecourse patterns.[12] During the past half century or so, there have been critical changes in regard to the social and economic roles of girls and women, the timing of crucial life events such as marriage, the overall pattern or shape of the lifecourse, and even the increased significance of and variation in the lifecourses of individuals (cf. Kohli 1986; Riley, Huber and Hess 1988; Worthman and Whiting 1987). Many indigenous customs have disappeared or been attenuated or replaced by new ideas, institutions, and ways of doing things: arranged marriages, the bride's virginity test, old people's beer groups, indigenous ceremonies (birth, infant naming, tooth removal, wedding, funeral). Daughters-in-law are likely to have greater autonomy, get their own kitchen earlier, or even be living in a city away from the mothers-in-law who might otherwise be their tutors. The very nature of work has changed, or rather, been added to, with the development of cash cropping, trading and wage labor. These and other lifecourse changes are summarized in Figure 2 (see Cattell 1989a for details; cf. LeVine and LeVine 1985; Ware 1984).

FIGURE 2
Changes in Abaluyia female lifecourse

Life stage	Grandmothers	Granddaughters
Fetus	Not discussed	Can be discussed
[Transition]	Birth	Birth
Newborn	Naming ceremony	Often omitted
Infant	Dependency, family care	Dependency, family care
Child	Learns about work	Learns about work
	Esibinje (GM* house)	Primary school
Youth	Tooth removal	KCPE* (8th grade) exam
Ripe (ready		Secondary school
to marry)	Sex, no intercourse	Premarital pregnancy
[Transition]	Marriage (arranged,	Marriage (by choice
	even forced)	and at later age)
	Indigenous ceremonies	None, or church wedding
Wife	Apprentice to MIL*	Greater autonomy
	Birth of children	Birth of children
	Work: subsistence	Work: peasant farming,
	farming, domestic	domestic work, wage
	work	labor, trading
		Urban experiences
		Head of household
Mature	Own kitchen; MIL* role	May get kitchen earlier
Old	Drank with beer group	Custom lapsed
	Customary rituals	Many rituals lapsed
	Full *amakesi* (wisdom)	Literacy competes
	Strong advisory role	Weaker role
	Economic peak	Young get wealth
	Greatest respect	Respect more widely distributed
	Widowhood & leviratic	Remarriage may be refused
	remarriage	
Very old	Return to dependency	Return to dependency
	and family care	and family care
[Transition]	Death	Death
Spirit	Indigenous rituals	Christian rituals
(ancestor)	GC* named for GM after	GC named for GM while
	GM's death	GM still living

* GC = grandchild; GM = grandmother; MIL = mother-in-law; KCPE = Kenya Certificate of Primary Education.
From Cattell 1989a: © Maria G. Cattell ALL RIGHTS RESERVED.

The changes in the relationships of grandmothers and granddaughters were neatly summed up by one old woman who told me: "Nowadays it isn't easy to advise the young". Advising – in the sense of imparting knowledge and providing moral and social guidance – has been a preeminent duty of older

Samia. But now "it isn't easy to advise", because young people want the knowledge of schools and books, which grandmothers lack. Hardly any women over the age of 50 had any formal schooling; they cannot read or write, some do not even count in the modern style. Often older women do not know what younger women want to know. For instance, preventing pregnancy is a topic of great interest to most young people. When grandmothers were young, a bride was expected to be a virgin (with a wedding night test of virginity) and a lengthy postpartum sex taboo was the norm. What girls want to talk about is "family planning" (modern, imported contraceptive means), which they can discuss among themselves because it would be a rare grandmother who possesses this knowledge.

As we have seen, in the past grandmothers were cultural experts who instructed and advised granddaughters in socially recognized settings such as *esibinje*. Their authority over granddaughters was moderated by the special relationship style they enjoyed – a style which probably facilitated the girls' learning. Today old women's cultural expertise and socially recognized authority have been badly eroded. While grandmothers and granddaughters enjoy each other's company and participate in exchanges of labor, knowledge, gifts, and affection, they clearly do so to a lesser extent than was possible a few decades ago.

Along with a decline in the value of many aspects of indigenous knowledge (Cattell 1989b), some of it the special province of older women, local concepts of cognitive ability may be giving way to Euroamerican definitions of intelligent behavior (Putman and Kilbride 1980). Thus not only valued knowledge, but even cognitive styles may be changing.

In addition, today's grandmothers, who themselves are aging and perhaps in need of assistance from their families, may have very heavy burdens, including responsibility for unmarried daughters' children. While grandmothers had childcare and socialization responsibilities in pre-modern times, the current boom in premarital pregnancies means that families must manage the stigma of the situation and grandmothers (especially maternal grandmothers) often accept responsibility for the child, even to the extent of earning money to pay school fees (Cattell 1989a; Khasiani 1985; Kilbride and Kilbride 1990, 1992; cf. Sangree 1986, 1992).[13]

The case study which follows illustrates some aspects of grandmother-granddaughter relationships in Kenya today. The case study is unusual in that it is most often the mother's mother who assumes responsibility for grandchildren born of premarital pregnancies. In addition, both the grandmother (father's mother) who raised Frankline and the granddaughter herself have been more successful than most of their respective age peers. However, the style of their relationship follows the Abaluyia ideal, and both Frankline's grandmothers, though differing in their own worldly achievements, are like many Abaluyia grandmothers in their hopes for their granddaughters' success in the modern world of formal education and wage employment – a world vastly different from the one in which their grandmothers grew up.

TWO GRANDMOTHERS AND THEIR GRANDDAUGHTER

with Frankline Teresa Mahaga[14]

Frankline was born in 1971. When her parents did not marry, she was left in the care of her mother's mother, Elizabeth – the usual arrangement in such cases. A few months later, to everyone's surprise, and to their criticism, Elizabeth took the baby to her father. "I did this", Elizabeth told Frankline in 1992, "because I thought you would have a better future. And you did, you have continued your education even up to university. If I had [not done that], you would not have gone far. You would be married and even having [my] grandchildren". Elizabeth is a peasant farmer who never went to school, though she became a certified midwife in later life.

Frankline's father, who was still in school, asked his mother Paulina to care for the child. In 1971 grandmother Paulina Ayiemba Mahaga, then in her late 40s, was a recent widow. As the senior wife of four, she was responsible for a large family: three junior co-wives and all their many children, including her own nine, most still young. She was also managing several businesses – hers and those developed by her deceased husband Fabianus Mahaga – in the small lakeside community of Port Victoria in Bunyala. A woman of great personal strength and determination, Paulina became, in effect, the managing director of a small family corporation. She managed the large family compound and the many people who lived in it, and continued to succeed in business. She saved money, bought land – and made sure her own and all her co-wives' children were educated. Unlike most women her age, Paulina had gone to school for a few years. Like Frankline's maternal grandmother, she was – and is – a great believer in education as the key to getting ahead in life.

Little Frankline quickly became Paulina's favorite. She was cared for by her father's younger sisters, then adolescents, and by housegirls and other employees of her grandmother. In the evenings she ate supper with her grandmother and they slept in the same room. Here Frankline recited accounts of her day, and Paulina listened and commented, supporting her granddaughter and advising her how to get along in the world. "My grandmother was so strict on education, and she taught me 'a-e-i-o-u' and how to count in English up to 5", said Frankline, "and she made sure my father got me books and pens. She also had me help her in her shop so I could begin learning business". Paulina also paid the fee so Frankline could attend nursery school.

In 1978 Frankline was enrolled as a boarder at Nangina Girls Primary School in Samia. Paulina paid the first year's school fees. Then Frankline's father, by now a successful business person like his parents, took over. But it was Paulina who came almost every Saturday to visit her granddaughter during school visiting hours, to see how her granddaughter was getting along and to make sure she did not lack for anything she needed. When Frankline was leaving for secondary school, again as a boarder, "the last person I saw was my grandmother, and she told me, 'You are going to a different place. You have to respect people'".

After Frankline finished secondary school she was admitted to a private university in Nairobi. Her family was unable to come up with the necessary tuition money, but with financial help from outside the family, Frankline went through. In June 1993 she received her B.A. in Business. The 'upcountry' grandmother who became her surrogate mother and was always Frankline's chief supporter and adviser was a proud observer at the commencement ceremonies. Frankline is now continuing her education in an M.B.A. course at the same university. In thus preparing herself for a business career she is following in Paulina's footsteps, in a modern transformation of her grandmother's business career – a transformation encouraged and approved by Paulina.

CONCLUSIONS

Among Abaluyia of western Kenya, 'grandmother' is one of a number of roles for older women. It is an important role in aging women's struggles to survive physically in what is for many an environment of material poverty, and in their struggles to survive as valued persons in a modern social realm marked by erosion of older persons' roles and opportunities to gain high status and accumulate material and social resources. Being a grandmother remains important for a woman's survival in both senses, and women as grandmothers continue to have valued family roles and significant connections with granddaughters. Grandmothers, often the ones who cope with children from premarital pregnancies (in yet another increase in rural women's workload), are also essential for family survival.

Indigenous ideals about grandmother-granddaughter relationships have persisted through the radical changes of the past century. In a social world of pervasive hierarchy, grandmothers' relationships with granddaughters play down status differences, foster emotional warmth, and facilitate the educational roles of grandmothers. For grandmothers who are becoming frail and in need of care, granddaughters often provide needed assistance in daily work. Grandmother-granddaughter relationships mediate relationships with other family members, especially an older woman's daughters and daughters-in-law. Granddaughters assure grandmothers of immortality, of the continuation of kinship roles and social recognition after the grandmother's death and transition to the spirit world.

In spite of enormous social change, in spite of increased experiential and psychological distances between the generations, many grandmothers and granddaughters in modern Kenya find both instrumental and expressive value in their relationships.

ACKNOWLEDGEMENTS

I am grateful for the invaluable help over the past decade of my Abaluyia field assistants, especially John Barasa 'JB' Owiti from Samia, who has been with me throughout, and, since 1985, Frankline Teresa Mahaga from Bunyala. Thanks also to the Medical Mission Sisters, Nangina Hospital, Nangina Girls Primary School, Nangina Mixed School and Sigulu Primary School, and Samia officials, among others; and to my husband Bob Moss. Above all, *mutio muno* to the many people of Samia and Bunyala who allowed me to share their lives in various ways. Research funds were provided by the National Science Foundation (grant BNS8306802), the Wenner-Gren Foundation (grant 4506), and Bryn Mawr College (Frederica de Laguna Fund grant). Portions of this article derive from an invited lecture on 'Women of Power: Age Hierarchies in Modern Kenya', given at Cleveland State University in June 1993.

NOTES

[1] Among the Tallensi of Ghana, for example, a grandson may marry the widow of any man he calls grandfather, except for his biological grandfather (Fortes 1949).
[2] For example, in East Africa, among Abaluyia of Kenya (Cattell 1989a; Kilbride and Kilbride 1990; Sangree 1966), Rendille pastoralists in Kenya (Spencer 1973), and Hehe of Tanzania (Brown 1935); and elsewhere in Africa, among !Kung foragers in Botswana (Biesele and Howell 1981), Lovedu of South Africa (Krige and Krige 1943), Mende of Sierra Leone (Bledsoe and Isiugo-Abanihe 1989), and Tallensi of Ghana (Fortes 1949).
[3] Abaluyia are concentrated in the Western Province of Kenya, consisting of three districts or counties, Bungoma, Busia and Kakamega. While I have visited the other districts, my rural fieldwork has been done primarily in southernmost Busia District.
[4] For fuller discussion of indigenous/precolonial Abaluyia life and the changes of the past century, see Burt (1978); Cattell (1989a, 1989b, 1992a); Moody (1967); Seitz (1978); Soper (1986); Thomson (1885). The "Samia Location" of the period researched by Seitz (1890–1930) included the present-day Samia and Bunyala Districts. Kitching (1980) has much general material on socioeconomic change in western Kenya and many details on Abaluyia areas. Wagner (1949, 1956), who did detailed research among the northern Abaluyia Bukusi and Maragoli groups in the 1930s, is often taken as the baseline study for all Abaluyia; for southern Abaluyia, he must be referred to cautiously.
[5] It is interesting to consider Caldwell's ideas about the upward direction (from children to parents) of 'wealth flows' in conjunction with Schatzberg's (1992) point that for Africans, power involves not only the control of resources (including people's labor), but their consumption, so that a person's fat body results from and is evidence of social and political power. When a Samia woman in her 80s said to me, "All we old people think about is eating", I took her statement literally. But it may bear thinking about in terms of losses of status and power experienced by the elderly.
[6] I never knew of a grandmother and granddaughter who were 'really' co-wives. In the same symbolic vein, a girl and her grandfather, and a boy and his grandmother, may call each other 'husband' and 'wife'.
[7] This idea will be explored in a paper in preparation for the 1994 annual meeting of the Society for Applied Anthropology: "Liminal Beings: Old People and Adolescents in Samia, Kenya".
[8] Of the 14 women with no grandchild, 5 were childless; most others without grandchildren were in the 50–59 age category. Table I keeps the data for grandfathers from the original table (in Cattell 1989a) so that readers may note the many similarities

between grandmother and grandfather roles and interactions with grandchild. Data for grandchildren were not collected by gender.

[9] Similar kinds of advice were given by about half the grandparents reported on in a 1984 survey of 155 seventh and eighth graders (77 girls, 78 boys) in Samia (see Cattell 1989a). Such advice is one aspect of elders' verbal promotion of proper behavior from juniors; the obverse is old people's complaints about not being treated properly (Cattell 1992c).

[10] Cohen (1985) describes the similar custom of Luo people in Siaya District, east of Samia. Young boys also slept in *esibinje* but as they approached adolescence they spent their evenings at the men's fire and slept in the cowshed. (My Samia friends tell me I have been misspelling the word for grandmother's house in earlier publications; *esibinje* is correct).

[11] Over half (55%) also reported having slept in their grandfather's house. In Samia homesteads, each married woman has her own house; in the past a man often had his own separate house, though that is less common today.

[12] Discussions of the lifecourse as a research focus and analytical framework include Elder (1985), Fry (1990), Fry and Keith (1982), Hagestad (1990).

[13] These problems are not peculiar to Abaluyia, to Kenya, nor to East Africa; they are found throughout subsaharan Africa (Gyepi-Garbrah 1985). Of 252 older women and men (a subsample of my larger survey), 29% said that they had at least one dependent grandchild in their home.

[14] Frankline "Terrie" Mahaga helped in the research for this case study and in the creation of this account of it. The case study is based on materials collected from 1985 to the present, including interviews with Frankline and both her grandmothers (some done by Frankline), and my own extensive participant observation with Frankline and her family.

REFERENCES

Albert, S.M. and M.G. Cattell 1994 Old Age in Global Perspective: Cross-Cultural and Cross-National Views. Human Relations Area Files Series: Social Issues in Global Perspective. G.K. Hall/Macmillan.

Apple, D. 1956 The Social Structure of Grandparenthood. American Anthropologist 58:656–663.

Apt, N.A. 1987 The Role of Grandparents in the Care of Children in Ghana. In Problems and Aspirations of Ghanaian Children: Implications for Policy and Action. P.A. Twumasi, ed. Pp. 264–291. Project Report for the Ghana National Commission on Children. Accra: Government of Ghana.

Bengtson, V.L. and J.F. Robertson, eds. 1985 Grandparenthood: Research Policy and Perspectives. Beverly Hills: Sage.

Biesele, M. and N. Howell 1981 "The Old People Give You Life": Aging Among !Kung Hunter-Gatherers. In Other Ways of Growing Old: Anthropological Perspectives. P.T. Amoss and S. Harrell, eds. Pp. 77–98. Stanford: Stanford University Press.

Blacking, J. 1990 Growing Old Gracefully: Physical, Social and Spiritual Transformations in Venda Society, 1956–66. In P.H. Spencer, ed. Anthropology and the Riddle of the Sphinx: Paradoxes of Change in the Life Course. Pp. 112–130. London and New York: Routledge.

Bledsoe, C. and U.C. Isiugo-Abanihe 1989 Strategies of Child Fosterage among Mende Grannies in Sierra Leone. In Reproduction and Social Organization in Sub-Saharan Africa. Ron Lesthaeghe, ed. Pp. 442–474. Berkeley: University of California Press.

Bohannan, P. 1959 The Impact of Money on an African Subsistence Economy. Journal of Economic History 19:491–503.

Brown, E.F. 1935 Hehe Grandmothers. Journal of the Royal Anthropological Institute

65:82–96.

Burt, E.C. 1978 Towards an Abaluyia Art History. University of Washington: Ph.D. dissertation.

Burton, L.M. 1992 Black Grandparents Rearing Children of Drug-Addicted Parents: Stressors, Outcomes, and Social Service Needs. The Gerontologist 32:744–751.

Caldwell, J.C. 1982 Theory of Fertility Decline. New York: Academic.

Cattell, M.G. 1989a Old Age in Rural Kenya: Gender, the Life Course and Social Change. Bryn Mawr College: Ph.D. dissertation.

Cattell, M.G. 1989b Knowledge and Social Change in Samia, Western Kenya. Journal of Cross-Cultural Gerontology 4:225–244.

Cattell, M.G. 1992a Praise the Lord and Say No to Men: Older Samia Women Empowering Themselves. Journal of Cross-Cultural Gerontology 7:307–330.

Cattell, M.G. 1992b Burying Mary Omundu: The Politics of Death and Gender in Samia, Kenya. Paper presented at the annual meeting of the African Studies Association, Seattle.

Cattell, M.G. 1992c Old People and the Language of Complaint: Examples from Kenya and Philadelphia. Paper presented at Language and Aging Pre-session, Georgetown University Roundtable on Languages and Linguistics, Washington DC.

Cohen, D.W. 1985 Doing Social History from Pim's Doorway. In Reliving the Past: The Worlds of Social History. Olivier Zunz, ed. Pp. 191–235. Chapel Hill: University of North Carolina Press.

Cronk, L. 1991 Wealth, Status, and Reproductive Success among the Mukogodo of Kenya. American Anthropologist 93:345–360.

Downs, V.C. 1992 Grandmothers and Granddaughters in African-American Families: Imparting Cultural Tradition and Womanhood between Generations of Women. Paper presented at Language and Aging Pre-Session, Georgetown University Round Table on Languages and Linguistics, Washington DC.

Elder, G.H., Jr., ed. 1985 Perspectives on the Life Course. In Life Course Dynamics: Trajectories and Transitions, 1968–1980. G.H. Elder, Jr., ed. Pp. 234–49. Ithaca, NY: Cornell University Press.

Drucker-Brown, S. 1982 Joking at Death: The Mamprusi Grandparent-Grandchild Joking Relationship. Man (n.s.) 17:714–727.

Foner, A. and D.I. Kertzer 1978 Transitions Over the Life Course: Lessons from Age-Set Societies. American Journal of Sociology 83:1081–1104.

Foner, N. 1984 Ages in Conflict: A Cross-Cultural Perspective on Inequality Between Old and Young. New York: Columbia University Press.

Fortes, M. 1949 The Web of Kinship among the Tallensi. Oxford University Press.

Fortes, M. 1984 Age, Generation, and Social Structure. In Age and Anthropological Theory. D.I. Kertzer and J. Keith, eds. Pp. 99–122. Ithaca, NY: Cornell University Press.

Fry, C. 1990 The life Course in Context: Implications of Research. In Anthropology and Aging: Comprehensive Reviews. R.L. Rubinstein, Pp. 129–149. Norwell, MA: Kluwer.

Fry, C.L. and J. Keith 1982 The Life Course as a Cultural Unit. In Aging and Society, Volume 3: A Sociology of Age Stratification. M.W. Riley, M. Johnson and A. Foner, eds. Pp. 51–70. New York: Russell Sage Foundation.

Gulliver, P.H. 1963 Social Control in an African Society. A Study of the Arusha: Agricultural Masai of Northern Tanganyika. Boston: Boston University Press.

Gyepi-Garbrah, B. 1985 Adolescent Fertility in Sub-Sahara Africa. New York: The Pathfinder Fund.

Hagestad, G.O. 1990 Social Perspectives on the Life Course. In R.H. Binstock and L.K. George, eds. Handbook of Aging and the Social Sciences. Third edition. Pp. 151–168. New York: Academic.

Ingstad, B., F. Bruun, E. Sandberg and S. Tlou 1992 Care for the Elderly, Care by the

Elderly: The Role of Elderly Women in a Changing Tswana Society. Journal of Cross-Cultural Gerontology 7:379–398.

Kerns, V. and J.K. Brown, eds. 1992 In Her Prime: New Views of Middle-Aged Women. Second edition. Urbana: University of Illinois Press.

Kertzer, D.I. and O.B.B. Madison 1981 Women's Age-Set Systems in Africa: the Latuka of Southern Sudan. In Dimensions: Aging, Culture, and Health. C.L. Fry, ed. Pp. 109–130. New York: Praeger.

Khasiani, S.A. 1985 Adolescent Fertility in Kenya with Special Reference to High School Teenage Pregnancy. Nairobi: The Pathfinder Fund.

Kilbride, P.L. 1986 Cultural Persistence and Socio-Economic Change among the Abaluyia: Some Modern Problems in Patterns of Child Care. Journal of East African Research and Development 16:35–51.

Kilbride, P.L. 1990 Adolescent Premarital Pregnancies Among Abaluyia of Kenya: The Grandparent Role. Paper presented at annual meeting of African Studies Association, Baltimore.

Kilbride, P.L. 1992 Unwanted Children as a Consequence of Delocalization in Modern Kenya. In Anthropological Research: Process and Application. John J. Poggie, Jr., Billie R. DeWalt and William W. Dressler, eds. Pp. 185–203. Albany: SUNY Press.

Kilbride, P.L. and J. Kilbride 1990 Changing Family Life in East Africa: Women and Children at Risk. University Park: Pennsylvania State University Press.

Kilbride, P.L. and J. Kilbride 1992 Stigma, Role Overload, and the Delocalization of Family Tradition: Problems Facing the Contemporary Kenyan Woman. Paper presented at Conference on Ecological and Cultural Change and Human Development in Western Kenya, Kakamega, Kenya.

Kitching, G. 1980 Class and Economic Change in Kenya: The Making of an African Petite-Bourgeoisie. New Haven: Yale University Press.

Kohli, M. 1986 The World We Forgot: A Historical Review of the Life Course. In Later Life: The Social Psychology of Aging. V.W. Marshall, ed. Pp. 271–303. Beverly Hills, CA: Sage.

Krige, E.J. and J.D. Krige 1943 The Realm of a Rain-Queen: A Study of the Pattern of Lovedu Society. London: Oxford University Press.

Legesse, A. 1973 Gada: Three Approaches to the Study of African Society. New York: The Free Press.

LeVine, S. and R.A. LeVine 1985 Age, Gender, and the Demographic Transition: The Life Course in Agrarian Societies. In Gender and the Life Course. A.S. Rossi, ed. Pp. 29–42. New York: Aldine.

Mayer, K.U. and W. Muller 1986 The State and the Structure of the Life Course. In Human Development and the Life Course. A.B. Sorensen, F.E. Weinert and L.R. Sherrod, eds. Pp. 217–246. Hillsdale, NJ: Lawrence Erlbaum Associates.

Mbiti, J.S. 1969 African Religions and Philosophy. Nairobi: Heinemann.

Minkler, M. and K.M. Roe 1993 Grandmothers as Caregivers: Raising Children of the Crack Cocaine Epidemic. Newbury Park, CA: Sage.

Møller, V. 1990 A Role for Black Seniors in Educare: A Community Assessment. Pretoria: Human Sciences Research Council.

Møller, V. 1992 Black South African Women on Excursions: A Reflection on the Quality of Township Life for Seniors. Journal of Cross-Cultural Gerontology 7:399–428.

Moody, R.W. 1963 Samia Fishermen. In East African Institute of Social Research Conference Proceedings. Pp. 1–9. Kampala, Uganda: Makerere University.

Moody, R.W. 1967 Social and Political Institutions of the Samia. University of Cambridge: M. Litt. Thesis.

Moore, S.F. 1978 Old Age in a Life-Term Social Arena. Some Chagga of Kilimanjaro in 1974. In Life's Career – Aging: Cultural Variations on Growing Old. B.G. Myerhoff and A. Simic, eds. Pp. 23–76. Beverly Hills, CA: Sage.

Pelto, P.J. 1973 The Snowmobile Revolution: Technology and Social Change in the

Arctic. Menlo Park, CA: Cummings.

Plath, D.W., ed. 1983 Work and the Lifecourse in Japan. Albany NY: State University of New York Press.

Poggie, J.J. and R.N. Lynch 1974 Concluding Comments. In Rethinking Modernization: Anthropological Approaches. J.J. Poggie and R.N. Lynch, eds. Pp. 353–375. Westport, CT: Greenwood.

Putman, D.B. and P.L. Kilbride 1980 A Relativistic Understanding of Intelligence: Social Intelligence among the Songhay of Mali and the Samia of Kenya. Paper presented at the annual meeting of the Society for Cross-Cultural Research, Philadelphia.

Radcliffe-Brown, A.R. 1940 On Joking Relationships. Africa 13:195–210.

Radcliffe-Brown, A.R. 1949 A Further Note on Joking Relationships. Africa 19:133–140.

Riley, M.W., ed. 1988 Sociological Lives: Social Change and the Life Course, Volume 2. Newbury Park: Sage.

Riley, M.W., B.J. Huber and B.B. Hess, eds. 1988 Social Structures and Human Lives: Social Change and the Life Course, Volume 1. Newbury Park: Sage.

Robertson, C. 1986 Social Change in Contemporary Africa. In Africa. 2nd ed. P.M. Martin and P. O'Meara, eds. Pp. 249-264. Bloomington: Indiana University Press.

Rosenmayr, L. 1988 More Than Wisdom: A Field Study of the Old in an African Village. Journal of Cross-Cultural Gerontology 3:21–40.

Rossi, A.S. and P.H. Rossi, eds. 1990 Of Human Bonding: Parent-Child Relations across the Life Course. New York: Aldine de Gruyter.

Sangree, W.H. 1966 Age, Prayer and Politics in Tiriki, Kenya. London: Oxford University Press.

Sangree, W.H. 1974 Youths as Elders and Infants as Ancestors: The Complementarity of Alternate Generations, Both Living and Dead, in Tiriki, Kenya, and Irigwe, Nigeria. Africa 44:65–70.

Sangree, W.H. 1986 Role Flexibility and Status Continuity: Tiriki (Kenya) Age Groups Today. Journal of Cross-Cultural Gerontology 1:117–138.

Sangree, W.H. 1992 Grandparenthood and Modernization: The Changing Status of Male and Female Elders in Tiriki, Kenya, and Irigwe, Nigeria. Journal of Cross-Cultural Gerontology 7:331–362.

Schatzberg, M.G. 1992 Power in Africa: A Cultural and Literary Perspective. Paper presented at the annual meeting of the African Studies Association, Seattle.

Seitz, J. 1978 A History of the Samia Location, 1890–1930. University of West Virginia: Ph.D. dissertation.

Soper, R. 1986 Kenya Socio-Cultural Profiles: Busia District. Nairobi: Ministry of Planning and National Development.

Spencer, P. 1965 The Samburu. A Study in Gerontocracy in a Nomadic Tribe. London: Routledge & Kegan Paul.

Spencer, P. 1973 Nomads in Alliance: Symbiosis and Growth among the Rendille and Samburu of Kenya. London: Oxford University Press.

Spencer, P. 1976 Opposing Streams and the Gerontocratic Ladder: Two Models of Age Organization in East Africa. Man 11:153–174.

Spencer, P. 1990 The Riddled Course: Theories of Age and Its Transformations. In Anthropology and the Riddle of the Sphinx: Paradoxes of Change in the Life Course. P.H. Spencer, ed. Pp. 1–34. London and New York: Routledge.

Stewart, F.H. 1977 Fundamentals of Age-Group Systems. New York: Academic.

Thompson, P. 1981 Life Histories and the Analysis of Social Change. In Biography and Society: The Life History Approach in the Social Sciences. D. Bertaux, ed. Pp. 289–306. Beverly Hills, CA: Sage.

Thomson, J. 1885 Through Masai Land. London: Edward Arnold.

Turner, V. 1969 The Ritual Process: Structure and Anti-Structure. Chicago: Aldine.

Udvardy, M. and M.G. Cattell 1992 Gender, Aging and Power in Sub-Saharan Africa: Challenges and Puzzles. Journal of Cross-Cultural Gerontology 7:275–288.

Wagner, G. 1949 The Bantu of North Kavirondo, Vol. I. London: Oxford University Press.

Wagner, G. 1956 The Bantu of North Kavirondo: Economic Life, Vol. II. London: Oxford University Press.

Wanjala, C.L. 1985 Twilight Years are the Years of Counsel and Wisdom. In History and Culture in Western Kenya: The People of Bungoma District through Time. S. Wandibba, ed. Pp. 78–91. Nairobi: Gideon S. Were Press.

Ware, H. 1984 Female and Male Life-Cycles. In Female and Male in West Africa. C. Oppong, ed. Pp. 6–31. London: George Allen & Unwin.

Weisner, T. 1992 Social Support and Family Change in Western Kenya. Paper presented at Conference on Ecological Change and Human Development in Western Kenya, Kakamega, Kenya.

Wood, V. and J. Robertson 1976 The Significance of Grandparenthood. In Time, Roles, and Self in Old Age. J. Gubrium, ed. Pp. 278–304. New York: Behavioral Publications.

Worthman, C.M. and J.W.M. Whiting 1987 Social Change in Adolescent Sexual Behavior, Mate Selection, and Premarital Pregnancy. Ethos 15:145–165.

WINIFRED L. MITCHELL

WOMEN'S HIERARCHIES OF AGE AND SUFFERING IN AN ANDEAN COMMUNITY

ABSTRACT. In the Aymara community of 'Utani', hierarchical relationships between middle aged and younger women are evident in the cycle of domestic life. An older woman – mother, sister, step mother, mother-in-law – has unquestioned authority as taskmistress over the labor of girls and young women; although very old women no longer wield such power. Post-marital residence patterns and the family life cycle contribute to the hierarchical relationships among women in an extended family household. When women's community-wide prestige is examined, however, a different pattern is apparent. Prestige among female peers is based less on age than on a woman's reputation for being long-suffering. The paper concludes that these two types of female hierarchy complement each other as part of women's adaptation to the exploitations of peasant life.

Key Words: female age hierarchy, Peru, Andes, Aymara women, Aymara aging

In the small Aymara community of Utani[1] in the Peruvian Andes, two types of female hierarchies are evident. First, the allocation of domestic work is based on the relationship of power and obligation between older and younger women who share kinship ties, whether consanguineal, affinal, or ceremonial. The second prestige system transcends age and work relationships and emphasizes women's long-suffering character. This informal, consensus-based hierarchy determines women's respect among female peers. These two types of hierarchy are complementary since both revolve around the concept of 'suffering woman-hood', which the first fosters and the second glorifies. Following a brief presentation of the Utani setting, women's personal narratives and community gossip data are used to describe these hierarchies.

UTANI

Utani is one of many similar villages dotting the rugged *altiplano* (high plain) surrounding Lake Titicaca. Its scattered sod houses with tin or thatched roofs are separated by tiny plots of agricultural or pasture land (see Figure 1). During my 1984 fieldwork, I lived among the 285 villagers, who comprised Utani's 55 households. Village landholdings are around 300 hectares, or slightly more than two and a half square kilometers. Families coax a living from their fields using labor intensive rainfall agriculture and careful animal husbandry. The land supports most of the people's subsistence needs with crops of potatoes, quinoa (a high protein grain), barley, and small herds of sheep, cattle, and other farm animals, but there is little surplus for sale. Droughts, floods, hail and frost are all possible impediments to successful farming, so families must be well organized and resourceful in managing production.

During the agricultural off-season, many Utani men migrate temporarily to

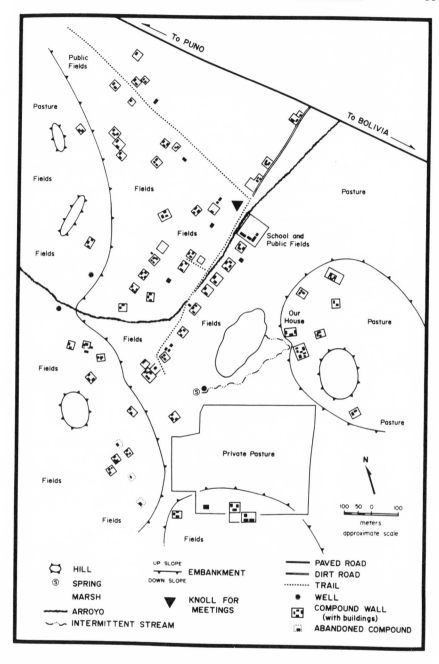

Figure 1. Map of Utani

the coastal cities and plantations for wage labor. The cash income from this
work supplements the family's subsistence living, usually generating the

equivalent of three to four hundred U.S. dollars a year. This cash buys a few staples and supplies, such as sugar, flour or kerosene, and modest consumer goods like radios, bicycles, and some manufactured clothing. Women also earn a little cash (U.S. $50.00 annually) from market activities, usually by buying and reselling goods such as fruit or wool on market days in town. When men migrate, women's responsibilities expand to cover the otherwise male tasks.[2] This situation of extra work for women that is created by men's absences belies the notion of an 'off-season'. Family members who remain at home always have plenty of work.

The yearly round of farming tasks occupies the time and energy of each household member. Particularly at planting and harvest, everyone is involved. Even absent household members often return to help out at the peak work times, with the possible exception of teenage boys and girls who cannot get away from their wage labor or domestic service jobs on the coast.

DOMESTIC WORK AND WOMEN'S RESPONSIBILITIES: THE *WARMI K'APAWA*

Work responsibilities are divided along gender lines, with much cultural emphasis on the interdependence and cooperation of spouses. Planting, cultivating, harvesting, and cash earning are male domains; and a woman only "helps with" but does not organize or get much credit for performing these tasks unless she is unmarried. Women's responsibilities include the household jobs of getting firewood, cooking, caring for children, washing, making and mending clothes, as well as raising farm animals. A woman may have to spend all day on a hillside spinning or knitting while supervising her livestock and children. Caring for animals is especially time-consuming during the early growing season. For example, in the spring, women gather grass and carry it to their livestock so they won't have to herd the animals to pasture through the fields of fragile young potato plants.

Women make a major contribution to agricultural labor, but Utani people consider agriculture a male activity. In 1984, when I listed women's and men's tasks (Mitchell 1986: 95–100), I found that women's responsibilities are more numerous and varied than men's. Women's work is more flexible to accommodate childrearing and the yearly fluctuations of agricultural labor demands, and their helpers are more numerous and varied in age than men's.[3] It is this delegation of female responsibility that gives the mother-of-the-family her authority over younger women in her household. She must exact help from her household's varied population of children and young adults to carry out her many jobs.

The domestic assignments with which older women dominate younger women's lives span the wide range of women's work in traditional Aymara peasant communities. Recalling their childhoods and young adulthoods, women describe their drudgery as young girls: cooking, herding sheep, caring for children, and performing tasks for relatives or neighbors to bring in extra resources for the family. The child's taskmistress is an older woman – mother, sister, stepmother, godmother, mother-in-law – who has unquestioned authority. For example, according to a middle-aged woman whom I will call Avelia:

> When my little sister was about so big [about four years old], my mother used to work the distant fields and leave me to care for my little sister all day in the house, just the two of us, and I was only a little bigger than she was. Once when my mother came home, there was nothing prepared for her to eat, and she asked me, "Why haven't you cooked? You are already a big girl [of six]". And she would beat me for something like that.

Avelia was only eight when her mother died, and these events are her outstanding memories of their relationship. Her accounts of subsequent treatment by stepmothers and aunts are no different. Similarly, Avelia's elderly mother-in-law, Victoriana told me:

> When I was a child, there was so much work to do. Sooooo much. That is why my hair is now gray. I cooked. I herded sheep, I cared for the babies. My family was poor and I was the oldest so I worked so hard!

Her account continues with a litany of jobs she performed from a young age for her household and neighbors to earn additional support for her family. For example, she earned extra barley by helping neighbors with their husking. Thus the family utilizes the labor of even the very young to make ends meet.

As mistress of her children's labor, a woman can ship a child or teenager off to work in another community to give service to relatives or *compadres*. The following account is by Vicenta, a young woman in her early twenties.

> When I was around eight years old, my mother sent me far away, to the other side of the hills, where my grandmother's sister lived. She loaned me to her. I would run away from there crying back home to my mother, but she would make me go back. They didn't give me anything; they didn't take care of me. They didn't even give me clothes to wear, nothing. During the rainy season I would get wet on the *pampa*, huddled up with the sheep, and I would just have to let my clothes dry on my body. That's how it was. They didn't even give me a change of clothes. I stayed there with them, herding their sheep, for over a year.

Vicenta is sent from one relative to another, and eventually works as a maid for her brother's godmother in the city of Puno. As an 'extra' child in a large family, her labor is most useful when loaned to another household.

When a new daughter-in-law enters the household, a mother-in-law can heap tasks on the bride and encourage her son to beat a young wife to help her learn obedience and diligence. Avelia, herself an exacting mother-in-law, had the following comments on her experiences in both sides of that relationship:

> My mother-in-law hated me because she said I didn't do any work and just spent all my time taking care of the baby....
>
> A good daughter-in-law shows respect to her mother-in-law. Sara was a wonderful daughter-in-law, always helping me and weaving beautifully, but Graciela is bad. She

just stays with her mother and never does any work for me. She doesn't even cook for her husband or bring the grandchildren to visit.

A woman who had been a captured bride[4] told me how her new mother-in-law and sister-in-law kept her occupied and locked up so that she would not be able to run away from her forced marriage. She nevertheless considered herself well-treated because she was not beaten as long as she worked hard and obeyed her new husband and in-laws.

There is a quality of desperation in the accounts of the never ending nature of work and the assignment and execution of women's tasks. "A *warmi k'apawa* – a hard working woman – is a respected woman", I was often told. There is so much work to be done that a "good woman's hands should never be idle. She should be seen from early morning to dusk at work and directing the work of her children." Her helpers are young children of both sexes, though boys become "little men" at age ten or twelve and begin working with their fathers in the fields. Daughters are heaped with their share of an adult woman's domestic responsibilities at an earlier age – seven or so, especially if they have numerous younger siblings.

Like temporary wage laborers, however, children are an intermittent source of help for a woman. They must be sent to school, leaving all their work for their mother to take over. Girls' education will be the first to be terminated if any stress limits the family budget or extra work is needed at home. Although mothers express a belief in the value of an education (which few of them have had), they are also eager to enlist their daughters' help at home before the girls' labor is lost to husbands and mothers-in-law.

MOTHER-OF-HOUSEHOLD'S AUTHORITY AND THE FAMILY LIFE CYCLE

Utani marriage and residence patterns are similar to those described for other Andean communities (Carter 1977; Albó 1976; Mayer 1977). Getting married is an extended process rather than a single event and usually begins with the young couple living together (*sirvisinya*) at one of their parents' homes. Virilocality is preferred, although neo- or uxorilocality are frequent choices due to amount of land, marital status of other siblings and simple compatibility with parents and in-laws. Of 26 fully married couples interviewed in Utani, 62% had begun their marriages living virilocally. Only one couple reported initial uxorilocality with the others saying that they had lived neolocally, either in Utani or on the coast.

If the *sirvisinya* relationship proves stable for two or three years, a couple establishes an independent nuclear family household. Thus, the *sirvisinya* period is a short window of an extended family household opportunity for an older woman to command the labor of an adult daughter or a daughter-in-law. The young bride must not be lazy. Though she may have a baby or two, she is expected not to spend all her time caring for the infants but to participate in all sorts of work under the older woman's direction. My observations suggest that the temporary nature of this parent-locality leads the older mother-of-household to pounce on these new brides and extract as much assistance from them as she can in the short time available. (Her demands might be comparable to those I would make if I were given a two-year gift subscription to a housekeeping service.)

I observed the arrival of a new bride who came to her husband's parents' home in Utani with her *sirvisinya* husband whom she had met while both were living in Puno, the department capital. Their marriage process began officially in Utani, where they were festively locked into a storeroom alone together for the night by the young husband's family. In the weeks that followed, the couple came from Puno for frequent visits to help with the harvest work. While the husband worked along with his brothers and father, the bride helped her new mother-in-law at every imaginable task. More clothes were washed and mended, tools polished, sheep sheared, potatoes sorted, and store rooms cleaned when the bride visited than at any other time. The mother-in-law was far more demanding of the bride than of her own teenaged daughter. The family had other married children living in Utani, a son and a daughter, but neither of the spouses was on good terms with them. In fact, they never spoke or came to the house. I wondered if the mother-in-law's exploitation of the new bride was so excessive that the young couple would soon be as alienated as her other married children were.

The current group of young parent-local newlyweds in Utani was mostly living uxorilocally (3 of 4 couples). This fact combined with the mother-in-law's behavior suggests that the mother-in-law taskmistress role may drive young couples to choose neo- or uxorilocal residence. Any parent-local bride would be expected to contribute considerable labor to the extended family household, but the daughters-in-law are more exploited. As Albó observes for the Bolivian Aymara, a high rate of village exogamy combined with virilocality also contributes to the exploitation or at least to the vulnerability of new brides (1976:6–15). In Utani, half of the married women were from outside the village, while only ten percent of the men were (a significant male-female difference, $p < 0.05$). As brides residing virilocally, these women would have been farther from their families' support and possibly more likly to be overworked by their mothers-in-law.

When her children are grown and established in independent households, a woman's status and independence will gradually decline with her increasing age until she remains with no apparent decision-making or labor-allocating power. Usually, she and her husband will live with or near their most compatible child (sons are preferred) who will gradually inherit their house and lands as they age, retire, and die. The two elderly Utani women (who reported their age in the eighties[5]) who were in this dependent position were strikingly passive. Both lived with their adult sons' families, one as a widow and the other with her somewhat senile husband. Both performed simple menial tasks such as spinning or gathering brambles for firewood but seemed to take little active interest in the affairs of the household. When I visited their families, they sat quietly in the background. One son referred to his parents in their presence as "worn out, ready to end their lives". The other son explained when I addressed a question to his mother, "She doesn't have any opinions", to which his mother agreed, "Yes, I really don't think much anymore". Their daughters-in-law (whom they probably once tyrannized) appeared indifferent to the older women's presence, showing them no special deference or attention.

These passive elders posed a puzzling contrast to the middle aged taskmistresses. Eight other Utani women (aged approximately 60–79, see note 5 above) appeared to be in transition between domineering independence and passive retirement. Six of these women lived with or very near married children, but no longer directed their labor. Most women or couples had a live-in grandchild (or in one case a great nephew) to help and keep them company, but the child's labor was not as exploitable as a new bride's. With all elderly people covered by one or both of these arrangements, no one is alone and unsupported in old age. These elders cannot, however, be described as occupying an automatic position of respect due to their ages. Instead, as their social contacts and power diminish, so does the attention and deference they receive from their families. This status transition fits the explanatory cross cultural aging model developed by Amoss and Harrell, who say that the status of the elderly rests on the balance between their contributions and the costs of maintaining them and also on the "degree of control the aged are able to retain" (1981:6).

EXPRESSION OF AGE HIERARCHIES IN INTER-HOUSEHOLD RELATIONSHIPS

Female kin obligations and networks are reinforced by an informal generalized reciprocity system (using Sahlins' 1972 terms). A woman sends or brings gifts of freshly butchered meat, milk, eggs or even bowls of cooked food to a female relative or agnate. This female networking is not considered the same as the more formal *ayni* (reciprocal labor exchange) relationship documented by many Andean scholars (e.g., Alberti and Mayer 1974; Bolton and Mayer 1977). In Utani, *ayni* is a male and/or head of household economic exchange, while women say of their reciprocity, "No it's not *ayni*, we just help each other." Such exchanges are informal markers of female hierarchical relationships because they are not strictly balanced. A more prosperous middle-aged woman will share more with an older or younger poorer relative, obligating that woman to repay her generosity, if not with comparable gifts then with labor, companionship, or a service such as weaving.

These generalized reciprocal exchanges are one of the few markers of female age hierarachy that extend beyond the household. Another is public deference shown by terms of address or by attention paid to one's remarks in a public meeting. Younger women defer to their older, more established peers, using honorific titles like '*Taika*' (mother) or '*Tia*' (aunt) regardless of their actual kin relationships.

In community affairs, I observed that younger and very old women are less likely to speak up in meetings than middle aged mothers-of-households, but there was no formal consensus among my informants on this point. They asserted that any adult can represent the household at community assemblies and can speak publicly as necessary.

In summary, the family, both in its nuclear and extended phases, lays the foundation for an age-based female hierarchy in this Aymara community. Authority and prestige differences revolve around the allocation of household tasks, but also apply to a generalized age respect system in inter-household relations. This age hierarchy is juxtaposed with the second respect system with which women gauge each others' long-suffering qualities.

THE PRESTIGE OF SUFFERING

Utani women display a noteworthy consensus about a hierarchy of suffering that transcends age, marital status, and kinship boundaries. While being hardworking (and obedient to one's overseers) is part of being a good woman, my informants explained to me that a woman should also be long-suffering and resourceful. She should be able to keep her family together against all the odds of Peruvian peasant life – poverty, illness, crop failure, death, and husbands who may be drunk, philandering, and/or abusive (see Mitchell 1993). When I asked women to rank each other according to respect, a significant consensus about this long-suffering prestige hierarchy was evident ($p < 0.001$, tested by Kendall's W [Siegel 1956: 237]). To obtain this information, I randomly divided my small group of female informants into subjects and judges, asking 15 judges to arrange Polaroid photographs of 16 subjects according to how much they respected each woman. Each judge sorted the photos independently, spreading them out on a cloth in her own courtyard and commenting liberally on all the subjects' current and past behavior, virtues and faults. Summaries of the accounts of a few subjects follow. They are listed in order of their pooled ranks, with Number 1 the highest:

Number 1: A 28 year old single woman whose *sirvisinya* had not resulted in a permanent marriage, probably due to her husband's philandering. She lives semi-independently, affiliated with her father's and young step-mother's household and earns a living in marketeering and contraband. She does not get along with her father's new wife but has no man of her own to help support her. She is a great hostess, conscientious mother, beautiful weaver, and a woman who speaks well and avoids controversy; but she suffers because of her single mother status. She is poor and pitted alone against the world.

Number 2: Referred to as '*taika*' by many peers, she is an elderly woman (over 60) who does healing ceremonies. She is described as working hard and being very poor since her husband spends most of his time on the coast and does not send much money home. She avoids controversy, speaks well and helps others.

Number 3: A young, unmarried woman in her early twenties, the head of a household of orphaned younger siblings. She is praised for her independence and coping skills. Managing a household and rearing her siblings without parents or husband earns her lots of respect for suffering. She is resourceful and popular though under some suspicion of having had a flirtation with a married man at a recent fiesta.

Number 4: An elderly married woman (65) who is described as peaceful, stay-at-home, hardworking. (I observed that she also dominates her live-in daughter-in-law, but no one commented on this.) She and her husband have suffered through some years of extreme poverty, for which she is respected.

Number 5: A prosperous middle aged married woman (40-ish) with 12 children. Everyone comments on how hard she works. She herself loves to talk about the suffering she endures with so many family responsibilities, and everyone seems to agree. Her hardworking qualities and those of her husband are touted as the reason for their prosperity.

The respect that these top ranked women receive is subtle but apparent in their peer interactions. These are women who are listened to; their opinions are sought in afternoon gossip; their conduct is an example for young girls; their quiet forbearance pervades community life.

As the descriptions of these top-ranked women show, age is not a predictor of this informal hierarchy. An equal mixture of old, middle-aged and young women occupy the middle ranks as well. These mid-ranked women are praised for being hardworking, tranquil and resourceful in coping with widowhood, violent and/or philandering husbands, or domineering mothers-in-law. Their faults include being contentious and perhaps overly independent. In one case a woman was frequently criticized for having had a flagrant affair with a married man and a battle with his wife.

Now, let us skip to the bottom of the respect hierarchy, where four middle-aged women receive unanimous sanction for flaws in their characters. Two cases are especially interesting:

Number 14: A 35-ish married woman who works hard to contribute to her family's prosperity. But she is believed to have had a child by another man while her husband was away on the coast. The baby died (or may have been killed, according to gossip), and the woman managed to patch things up with her husband – a point in her favor when she is compared to the fifteenth ranked woman.

Number 15: A 32 year old widow who describes herself as old, tired, hopeless and filled with suffering. However, she is unanimously condemned by her peers for being generally lazy, contentious, and unforgiving and for "killing her husband" (see Mitchell 1993). The core of her misbehavior was that she had caught her husband in a compromising situation with a neighbor woman and refused to forgive him or allow him to return to her house. A fight occurred during the confrontation between wife, husband, and mistress, and the man was hit on the head. No one seemed to know or care who struck the blow, but the wife was guilty because she forced him to wander the countryside, where he eventually died after deliberately or accidentally drinking a nasty pesticide called aldrine.

The woman who is ranked fifteenth was always criticized for her failure to keep her marriage intact and her overall feistiness. Her rank is consistently worse than Number 14, above, whose marriage did not fail even though she was an adulteress. Similarly, the neighbor woman/mistress of the same conflict is up in the middle ranks, where she is neutrally described as a hard worker, though a little bit wild. It thus appears that being an adulteress is not as bad for one's reputation as being an unforgiving wife.

The prestige of suffering is a hard won status for Utani women. One may suffer in all sorts of ways, from being overworked as a child or a young bride to being abused or abandoned at any time in the uncertain progress of adult life. Utani women say, "A girl is only born to suffer." But her flexibility and persistence determine her standing among her peers. She must manage to be hardworking and resourceful but not too independent if she wants to earn respect.

CONCLUSION

I was not surprised to learn that these female hierarchies exist in Utani. Writers like Rosaldo (1980) and Hrdy (1981:189–190) convinced me that it is reasonable to expect such hierarchies to be present among women. (The concern of peasant women with earning respect has also recently been well documented by Stephen, 1991.) I was, however, surprised to learn that the basis for prestige among one's peers is not the productivity of these hardworking women but their quality of being long-suffering. In other words, although a woman may be a well organized, productive and prosperous mother-of-household, she will not gain the full respect of her peers unless she suffers (and puts up with it). If we just looked at the taskmistress interactions within domestic units, only the dominance of older women over younger would be apparent, and the outcome of household prosperity would appear from our capitalist perspective to be the obvious basis for female prestige. In fact, in Utani, men's prestige, far more than women's, is tied to their productivity and prosperity, even though both sexes contribute much to the labor of the household. (See Mitchell 1986.)

The reputation rankings and the work allocation heirarchy combine to give us a picture of a woman's life in Utani. A girl is prepared early in life for her long-suffering, compliant role. As a little girl, she is assigned adult housekeeping, nurturing and herding responsibilities and must fulfill her obligations as well as her childish talents allow. She may be sent away at a young age to cope with work in a world where she cannot even rely on familial affection. As a bride, she will need to have mastered all the variety of domestic and farming skills that her mother-in-law and new husband will expect of her. When she reaches mother-of-household status, she takes on the responsibilities of taskmistress and manager for the assistants that come and go through her life and fills in for them when they are absent. For learning these coping skills and keeping her family functioning as a productive household unit, she gains the respect of her peers.

Although the prestige of suffering resembles the larger *ladino* society phenomenon of *marianismo* (Stevens 1973), there are some noteworthy differences. The Utani concept is not the same as the fully developed "cult of female spiritual superiority" described by Stevens (1973:90). While women certainly feel that they suffer at the hands of men, a woman's suffering prestige can also come from poverty, illness, excessive child bearing and rearing, or other life circumstances. Furthermore, Utani women do not compare themselves to men. They see themselves as neither spiritually superior nor economically inferior, just separate: different, though complementary. Nor did any of my informants ever compare herself or her suffering to that of the Virgin Mary. In fact, the folk Catholicism of Utani seems nearly devoid of this major doctrinal refinement, concentrating instead on more earth mother (*pache mama*) female deity imagery. In short, while some aspects of the prestige of suffering may be the result of acculturation to *ladino* culture, the Utani system has its distinct character, developed during centuries of the villagers' status as an exploited peasantry.

I think that the counterpoint of productive males and suffering females is related to the Aymara adaptation to exploitation by state society. It is often argued that such exploitation results in greater emphasis on the male as the producer and head of family since his is the most convenient labor to exploit (Blake 1974; Sacks 1975 and 1976; Wallerstein 1984). The gender attitudes observed in Utani are compatible with this interpretation. Women's age hierarchies reproduce and provision the household by organizing labor; the prestige of suffering glorifies and justifies this female role. It also perpetuates the male role as the interface between households and state society by keeping female prestige tied to putting up with suffering and keeping the household going in the face of all odds. Utani women do not vie with their men for recognition as producers or cash earners perhaps because they are satisfied with their peer-based prestige of suffering. To the foreign feminist observer, this prestige system may seem like an affirmation of an undesirable status quo; but it may be a satisfactory or at least satisfying adaptation to centuries of peasant status. The Aymara girl, born to suffer, is dominated by her elder taskmistresses until she gets her own turn at juggling her meager resources and allocating the sporadic labor of her family unit. If she succeeds at suffering, her peers' respect may be her reward.

ACKNOWLEDGEMENTS

The research on which this paper is based was funded jointly by the Inter American Foundation and the Fulbright Commission. The assistance and support of both are gratefully acknowledged. The comments of my friend and colleague, Barbara Feezor-Stewart, on the first draft of this paper are also much appreciated; so are the suggestions of the editors of this special issue. Finally and as ever, I am indebted to the people of 'Utani' for their friendship and cooperation with this study.

NOTES

[1] 'Utani' is a fictitious name derived from the Aymara phrase meaning "at home." This usage protects the privacy of my informants, whose names are also changed in the text.

[2] This phenomenon is noted by many peasant and development studies. For example,

Deere (1978) discusses it for Northern Peru; and Chaney (1980: 16–17) for numerous development-migration contexts.

[3] The Aymara division of labor is typical of the worldwide patterns described by Ember and Ember (1985: 286) and Brown (1970).

[4] Bride capture – abducting a woman by her would-be husband – occurs occasionally throughout the Andean region, though it may be less common now than in previous generations (e.g. see Bourque and Warren's discussion of forced marriages, 1981: 99–100). In this Utani case, the young woman, who was unused to drinking, was plied with cane alcohol by her uncle and his young male friend until she became unconscious. The friend then carried her off on his donkey to his own community a day's walk away. The informant was an elderly woman who said capturing was less common now than in her youth. I had learned that Aymara women do not like to discuss sexual matters, so I did not ask her at what point in such a relationship sexual relations ensue. Whatever the details, the marriage endured for life and was subsequently formalized with a church wedding.

[5] Reported ages for all Utani women are very approximate. In comparing my data with information about the same people gathered ten years earlier by Paul Brown (unpublished data collected for Brown 1978), I have noticed that people's reported ages increased by as little as two or three years and as much as fifteen in the ten year period. Thus, the numbers refer to more subjective categories: eighty is 'very old'; sixties and seventies are 'pretty old'; and the fifties are a time of transition between the child rearing and the retirement phases of life. The women I have called 'middle aged taskmistresses' mostly reported their ages in the forties and early fifties. There are some exceptions, however. For example, one widow told me she was "old and tired" and reported her age as 34.

REFERENCES

Alberti, G. and E. Mayer, eds. 1974 Reciprocidad e Intercambio en los Andes Peruanos. Peru Problema 12. Lima: Instituto de Estudios Peruanos.

Albó, J. 1976 Esposos, Suegros y Padrinos entre los Aymaras. In Esposos, suegros y padrinos entre los Aymaras, 2nd ed. J. Albó and M. Mamani, eds. Pp. 1–36. La Paz, Bolivia: Cuadernos de investigación del Centro de investigación y promoción del campesinado.

Amoss, P.T. and S. Harrell, eds. 1981 Other Ways of Growing Old: Anthropological Perspectives. Stanford, CA: Stanford University Press.

Blake, J. 1974 The Changing Status of Women in Developed Countries. Scientific American 231: 136–147.

Bolton, R. and E. Mayer, eds. 1977 Andean Kinship and Marriage. Washington, D.C.: American Anthropological Association Special Publication No. 7.

Brown, J.K. 1970 A Note on the Division of Labor by Sex. American Anthropologist 72: 1073–1078.

Brown, P.F. 1978 Fuerza por Fuerza: Ecology and Culture Change among the Aymara of Southern Peru. Ph.D. Dissertation, University of Colorado at Boulder.

Bourque, S.C. and K.B. Warren 1981 Women of the Andes: Patriarchy and Social Change in Two Peruvian Towns. Ann Arbor, MI: University of Michigan Press.

Carter, W.E. 1977 Trial Marriage in the Andes? In Andean Kinship and Marriage. R. Bolton and E. Mayer, eds. Pp. 177–216. Washington, D.C.: American Anthropological Association Special Publication No. 7.

Chaney, E. 1980 Women in International Migration: Issues in Development Planning. Washington, D.C.: United States Agency for International Development.

Deere, C.D. 1978 The Development of Capitalism in Agriculture and the Division of Labor by Sex: A Study of the Northern Peruvian Sierra. Ph.D. Dissertation, University of California at Berkeley.

Ember, C.R. and M. Ember 1985 Anthropology, 4th ed. Englewood Cliffs, New Jersey: Prentice Hall.

Hrdy, S.B. 1981 The Woman that Never Evolved. Cambridge, MA: Harvard University Press.

Mayer, E. 1977 Beyond the Nuclear Family. In Andean Kinship and Marriage. R. Bolton and E. Mayer, eds. Pp. 60–80. Washington, D.C.: American Anthropological Association Special Publication No. 7.

Mitchell, W.L. 1986 Male and Female Counterpoint: Gender Relations in an Andean Community. Ph.D. Dissertation, University of Colorado at Boulder.

Mitchell, W.L. 1993 Lightning Sickness. Natural History 102 (11): 6–8.

Rosaldo, M.Z. 1980 The Use and Abuse of Anthropology: Reflections on Feminism and Cross-Cultural Understanding. Signs: Journal of Women in Culture and Society 5(3): 389–417.

Sacks, K. 1975 Engels Revisited: Women, the Organization of Production and Private Property. In Toward an Anthropology of Women. R. Reiter, ed. Pp. 211–234. New York: Monthly Review Press.

Sacks, K. 1976 State Bias and Women's Status. American Anthropologist 78: 565–569.

Sahlins, M. 1972 Stone Age Economics. Chicago: Aldine.

Siegel, S. 1956 Nonparametric Statistics for the Behavioral Sciences. New York: McGraw-Hill.

Stephen, L. 1991 Zapotec Women. Austin, TX: University of Texas Press.

Stevens, E.P. 1973 Marianismo: The Other Face of Machismo in Latin America. In Female and Male in Latin America. A. Pescatello, ed. Pp. 89–102. Pittsburgh, PA: University of Pittsburgh Press.

Wallerstein, I. 1984 Household Structures and Labor Force Formation in the Capitalist World Economy. In Households in the World Economy. J. Smith, I. Wallerstein and H.-D. Evers, eds. Pp. 17–22. Beverly Hills, CA: Sage.

OLD WOMEN AT THE TOP
AN EXPLORATION OF AGE STRATIFICATION
AMONG BENA BENA WOMEN

ABSTRACT. The choices and opportunities of Bena Bena women of the Eastern Highlands Province of Papua New Guinea in both a pre-contact and contemporary context were shaped by systems of both age and gender stratification. This paper explores both the past and contemporary nature of this hierarchical system and considers how various cultural patterns created differences in the lives of younger and older women. This differentiation meant that older women had greater access to valued social roles and rewards, had increased authority within their households and played crucial roles in the education and ritual transformation of younger men and women. Culture change and economic development have altered the lives and activities of Bena Bena women in various ways. The differential access of women to these new opportunities is now the basis for a new system of age stratification in which older women occupy the top rung.

Key Words: women, age stratification, development, Papua New Guinea, Eastern Highlands

INTRODUCTION

Between February 1983 and May 1984 I resided in the Upper Bena Bena village of Ganaga located in the Eastern Highlands Province of Papua New Guinea. One of the things that I observed during my 15 month stay in Ganaga was a major difference in the lives and opportunities of younger and older women. Older women were involved in a greater variety of roles than younger women and also played a prominent role in newly introduced economic activities and organizations. In the following paper I will explore some of the factors/variables that may account for this pattern.[1]

BACKGROUND

It is generally agreed that all known cultures divide the individual life course into a series of stages (Keith 1985). Scholars interested in the anthropology of aging women have explored how women's lives change as they become older and enter the later stages of the life course. It is generally agreed that, cross-culturally, increased age brings role discontinuity to women and allows them to become more dominant and powerful. There are numerous ways in which role discontinuity brings improvement to older women's lives (Brown 1982; Brown, Kerns, and Contributors 1985; Cool and McCabe 1983; Counts 1984; Counts and Counts 1985; Kerns and Brown 1992). First, older women experience fewer restrictions on their behavior and mobility. For example, menopause and the cessation of menstrual taboos expands the opportunities of women in some cultures. Second, increased age and successful performance of culturally appropriate activities afford women greater ability to exert authority over husbands and other kin. Particularly relevant here is a woman's ability to allocate the labor of younger women in both her household and domestic group. Finally, in some cultures, older women have the opportunity to participate in extra-domestic roles. For example, some older women may take on roles as midwives and curers or have important roles to play in initiation and other specialized rituals involving both men and women. These changes with age create differences between the lives of older and younger women and can form the basis for female age stratification.

According to Foner (1984a:xi), age stratification exists in any society when "individuals in a society, on the basis of their location in a particular age stratum, have unequal access to valued social roles and rewards." This inequality can create tension between younger and older women. Particularly relevant here are Foner's ideas regarding the sources of inequality among women. This stratification develops between younger and older women as older women "acquire considerable domestic authority, gain prestige in the family and community and become more active in the public sphere" (1984a:240–241). This privileged position of older women may, in fact, allow them to exert some control over the lives and opportunities of younger women.

Though not a focus for anthropologists interested in the effects of change and development on women, scholars interested in the anthropology of aging agree that native concepts and systems of age can influence the outcome of the development process. Again Foner (1984b:212) found that change and development can interact with and affect traditional systems of age stratification. In short, the way individuals respond to change may depend upon their location in a system of age inequality.

The theoretical background outlined above has informed my understanding and analysis of how age inequalities affected both the past and contemporary lives of women in a Papua New Guinean community. The way of life of the Bena Bena of the Eastern Highlands community of Ganaga has been transformed in the span of 60 years. Women and their opportunity structure have been affected by both pre-contact systems of age and gender stratification and the nature of the local development process. In order to understand the choices and opportunities of contemporary Ganaga women, then, we must first explore how concepts of age and gender affected Bena Bena women in the pre-contact situation.

PRE-CONTACT GANAGA

To date much of the literature on the nature of pre-contact social relations in the Highlands of Papua New Guinea has focused on the stratified or unequal gender relations between men and women (Allen 1967; Brown and Buchbinder 1976; Faithorn 1976; Feil 1978; Hays and Hays 1982; Josephides 1985; Keesing 1982; Lederman 1986; Meggitt 1964; M. Strathern 1972). In most instances the lives and interests of men as a group have been contrasted or opposed hierarchically to the lives and interests of women as a group. Only rarely has age been seen as a source of inequality in Highlands social relations and in these few cases analysis has focused on the nature of traditional age stratification among men. In these cases, men as a differentiated group are contrasted or opposed to women as an undifferentiated or homogeneous group (Gelber 1986; Godelier 1982; Modjeska 1982; A. Strathern 1982). More recently, Marilyn Strathern (1987, 1988) has suggested that the preoccupation of Highland ethnographers with gender inequality has masked the presence of other sources of inequality such as age.

My understanding of pre-contact life in Ganaga was acquired through interviews with key informants of both sexes. This interpretation also benefitted from other comparative insights drawn from other anthropological research on the Bena Bena (Keil 1974; Keil and Johannes 1974; Young 1974). Langness' work (1964a, 1964b, 1967, 1969, 1971, 1974) was especially informative concerning male cult activity and gender ideology.

The Bena Bena refer to pre-contact times as 'the fighting time'. During this period, the Bena Bena participated in sweet potato horticulture, pig and cassowary husbandry, regional partner to partner fixed equivalent trade, and life course exchanges. Endemic warfare based on the bow and arrow and organized through Big-Man leadership were also key features of pre-contact life. Members of each of the three patrilineal clans resided together in a separate fortified hamlet that was strategically located for defensive purposes.

During the 'fighting time' both gender complementarity and gender and age inequality affected the lives of men and women. One aspect of gender ideology emphasized the stratified or unequal relation between men and women. According to informants, women were characterized as weak, wild, inconsistent and at times threatening. Women could be threatening because they could contaminate or pollute men and society with menstrual and childbirth fluids. Men were viewed as intelligent, strong and single-minded. It is important to note that men believed that their 'natural' strength could only be maintained through membership in a secret *nama* male cult (Langness 1967, 1974).

These 'natural' abilities of men and women affected the kinds of tasks they were assigned in the division of labor. Women's abilities were most appropriate for specific tasks in the activities of sweet potato horticulture, animal husbandry, household maintenance, and the raising of children. Men performed some horticultural tasks but their primary activities were based in warfare, exchange, and leadership. Their activities were viewed as superior to women's activities because it was through such activities as exchange and leadership that persons gained prestige and renown. This aspect of the pre-contact ideology of gender among the Bena Bena, then, stressed that a hierarchical relationship existed among men and women.

It was within the marital relationship that men and women could best perform their culturally appropriate activities (see also Langness 1969). These activities also contributed toward the building of a man's 'name'. The achievement of a 'name' was only possible when a husband and wife settled down and cooperated with one another. The most important roles for a Bena Bena woman were those of wife and mother and within these roles she was expected to support the activities of her husband, thus sharing his 'name'. The actual division of labor that structured daily life then stressed the ideological complementarity and interdependence of men and women.

When women reached menopause the ideological and behavioral differentiation between men and women became less clear. Post-menopausal women were more positively evaluated and could become involved in some extra-domestic activities because they were no longer capable of contaminating others. The changing activities and evaluations of postmenopausal women suggests that concepts of gender were in part grounded in the control of such vital substances as blood and semen (see also Meigs 1976, 1983). When women reached menopause their behavior was no longer affected by taboos that were concerned with protecting society from female pollution.

A person's age also affected the kinds of roles and activities that were considered culturally appropriate for them. The Bena Bena believed that an individual's life could be divided into a series of stages or categories. Individuals were viewed as members of a certain category based not on their chronological age but on their personal achievements and role performance. Below I will explore how a woman's opportunity structure changed as she moved through the life course and consider some of the ways in which age stratification afforded older women the opportunity to exert control over the lives and choices of younger women.

Younger Women

The category here called younger woman subsumes the female life course categories of Young Woman (Yafanae), Newly Married Woman (Yafaye), and Married Woman (Ae). After first menstruation rites, negotiations could begin for a young woman's marriage. Young men and women had virtually no say in the choice of their marriage partner in pre-contact times. While a young woman's male relatives, guardian and Big-Man found a husband for her, she enjoyed a period of freedom during which she attended formal courting parties. Prior to this period young girls assisted their mothers in horticultural production, animal husbandry, domestic maintenance, and childcare.

During her first month of residence in her husband's community, the new bride was not required to work. This was considered a time during which the bride and her new relatives could get to know one another. In fact her husband's relatives would prepare a large, new piece of land and contribute plants to the bride's wedding garden. A man from her husband's 'clan' also appointed himself 'brother of the bride' and took on some of the responsibilities of the bride's own brother or guardian (Young 1974:161). New brides (Yafaye) could not have sexual relations with their husbands until wives had been found for all of a man's agemates. During this period (two months-three years), a new bride resided with her mother-in-law and assisted her in horticultural and animal husbandry tasks. This was a particularly stressful situation because a bride's mother-in-law and other older women in the community were constantly judging the bride's abilities and qualities to ensure that she was worthy of the bridewealth given for her. This early period of marriage was also a difficult transition because most young women were forced to leave their natal communities and live with strangers.

A woman began to cohabit with her husband after he built a house for her in his parents' hamlet. After this transition she was considered a Married Woman (Ae). The early years of marriage were very difficult for a young couple. The man and wife were virtual strangers and the activities of warfare and male cults gave the couple few opportunities to get to know one another. Older members of the community pressured the young couple to settle down and begin working as a team, and this pressure often resulted in wife beating.

When a young couple finally settled down in their marriage, they could then begin their complementary tasks in production, reproduction, and exchange. Apart from very occasional participation in communal work parties, women performed their tasks individually. The production of children relieved some of the pressure exerted on the woman and allowed her to create a place for herself in her husband's community.

Older Women

The category older women includes the Bena Bena life course categories of Adult (Aloopae) and Old Woman (Litane). Bena Bena women were regarded as social adults when they reached menopause and when their successful role performance as wives and mothers reflected their commitment and responsibility to their husbands' and their husbands' community. Post-menopausal women were afforded more opportunities to participate in extra-domestic affairs because they were no longer capable of polluting others. Some of my male informants said that post-menopausal women were "more like men." Women, however, did not cross over and perform the activities of the opposite gender (Counts and Counts 1985; Poole 1981). The onset of menopause alone did not make one a social adult. Both physical changes and one's personal accomplishments affected the partial role shift from ascribed to achieved activities that came with social adulthood.

A woman's authority within her household increased when she became an adult. First, she controlled the labor of her unmarried daughters. Mothers-in-law had only limited control over daughters-in-law while daughters-in-law lived in the older women's house. Once a man built a house for his wife, and they began to cohabit, women performed their domestic activities alone. With sexual segregation adult women, in effect, headed their own households and directed, organized and controlled the labor of younger women. Older women also had more influence and control over decisions concerning the allocation of the fruits of their labor because they had demonstrated their abilities in animal husbandry horticulture.

)lder women also gained access to extra-domestic activities. First, they had a ιυ.ε to play in male initiation. Women provided food to male cult members while they initiated young boys. The wife of one of the older male initiators would be chosen to observe the purificatory rituals performed on the young boys.

Older women also performed rituals to celebrate the maturity and change in status of females in their 'clans'. During female initiation older women performed rituals to enhance the growth and strength of young girls. They also transferred important knowledge to the initiates about their "natural abilities" and culturally appropriate roles.

Older women also organized and controlled rituals to celebrate a girl's first menstruation. Young women were taught how to cleanse themselves and were educated about the taboos that would affect their behavior until menopause. During these times women were exempt from productive duties and would have to reside in the communal women's house. Most women viewed their confinement during menstruation and childbirth as a period of freedom from work and as a time to gossip and enjoy the companionship of other women. It is also likely that initiation rituals and coresidence in the women's house encouraged some solidarity among women because they represented one of the few or only contexts in which women acted together. In fact, some older women told me that they would lie about having their periods so that they could spend some time with their friends in the women's hut. Co-residence in the women's hut was also a context in which older women could encourage younger women to improve their role performance. Finally, older women also gave younger women further training in the activities associated with their primary roles. This included information on the informal power that women could wield against men. She could exercise this power through the manipulation of taboos, the purchase of sorcery, the withholding of productive labor and sexual access, and the use of magic and plants in abortion and birth control.

While it is probable that women did not completely share the male-dominated aspect of the gender ideology of their culture, they did agree on the inherent power and danger of their vital essences. It appears that older women played an active and complementary role in perpetuating a hierarchical ideological system by cooperating with men in male initiation and by educating young women in female initiation.

While it is impossible to reconstruct past ideology, it is possible that older women's involvement in the transmission of this ideology was fueled by various motives. On the one hand, through ritual education young women became aware of the nature of female reproductive power and the ways that this power could be manipulated (Dickerson-Putman 1993). In this sense this knowledge could be said to contribute to the empowerment of women. On the other hand transmission of this knowledge laid the basis for the age differentiation that brought greater choice and opportunity to the lives of post-menopausal women.

Ethnographic data from the Middle East seem to offer a parallel example of this later motivation. In her study of a Bedouin group, Lila Abu-Lughod (1986) found that menstruation and a woman's sexuality were both viewed in a negative way. Menstruation, as a natural force over which women had no control, represented pollution, inescapable weakness, and lack of self control. Women in fact were viewed as unclean until they reached monopause (Abu-Lughod 1986:131). A woman's sexuality was potentially threatening to the male-oriented social order and so women protected society by wearing the veil. By veiling themselves Bedouin women contributed to the perpetuation of a male moral order they undoubtedly helped to create. It is generally agreed that older Bedouin women educate younger women about how to cleanse themselves after menstruation and sexual activity and enforce the veil's proper use (Abu-Lughod 1986:159). Women wear the veil less as they grow older. Abu-Lughod notes (1986:163) that:

> As elders themselves, these women, who have been responsible for rearing these young men, become more identified with the social system. They are more like men and aspire to the moral virtues of assertiveness, self-control, and piety that justify men's positions in the hierarchy.

Similarly, among the pre-contact Bena Bena, older women no doubt joined with men in supporting, maintaining, and reproducing an ideological system that included customs such as taboos and female initiation in an effort to protect their privileged position and keep young women in their place.

Adult women also had the opportunity to achieve positions outside the household. Some women achieved renown as midwives and curers. As female curers, older women monopolized knowledge concerning the use of plants and spells for conception, abortion and contraception. Midwives were women whose expertise concerning difficult births was widely respected. Both curers and midwives were paid by patients for their services.

The most prominent role an adult woman would achieve outside the household was that of Big-Woman (Gipinae). This women might have been the wife of a Big-Man but not necessarily so. She was a person that the other women trusted; she was beyond her child-bearing years, was renowned for her horticultural and animal husbandry skills, had given birth to many children, and was a capable speaker. All of the women in a 'clan' designated one woman to represent their interests and perspectives within the community. A Big-Woman also helped to organize and orchestrate the rituals associated with female initiation and generally acted as an advisor to women.

When an adult woman began to move slowly, and when she became very gray haired, she was called Old Woman (Litane). As it became obvious to the community that an old woman could no longer care for herself, a caretaker was chosen either by the person herself or her son (Langness 1967:71). The caretaker saw to it that the *Litane* did not lack for necessities such as food and firewood.

Summary

The discontinuity in the lives of old women created age inequalities in the activities and opportunities of older and younger women. Older women were at the top in this system of stratification because they had more access to the socially more important extra-domestic roles. Older women also affected the choices, opportunities, and knowledge of younger women. An examination of female initiation revealed the educational and ideological control that older women exerted over younger women.

CONTEMPORARY GANAGA

In a period of 60 years the Bena Bena have been transformed into coffee-producing peasants (Dickerson-Putman 1986; Finney 1973). Income-earning activities are considered "bisnis" and are afforded high cultural value. One new and important "bisnis" activity for women is participation in producer-seller markets. Various investment-based activities have also been introduced. The Papua New Guinea Government's concern with the role of women in development has led to the creation of various women's clubs and corporations (Dickerson-Putman 1986; Sexton 1982; Schoeffel-Melissea 1987). Although high cultural importance is placed on "bisnis," a household's primary responsibility is to meet the needs of its members through horticultural production and animal husbandry.

Culture change and development have molded a new world for the residents of Ganaga. The contemporary community of Ganga consists of 87 households (347 people) dispersed over 17 named territories/hamlets. Sixteen (18.3%) of these households are members of the Seventh Day Adventist Church. There is also a Community School where children can attend grades one through six. Two other recent components of contemporary Ganaga are a Health Post and a formal market area located on the edge of the community. Ganaga was also the site for one of the three women's investment corporations in the Eastern Highlands (Dickerkson-Putman 1986, 1990).

Women's roles in and ideological association with production have changed little since pre-contact times because development has stressed export and not domestic production. Most Ganaga women plant newly introduced cultigens which they then sell in producer-seller markets. The workload of woman has increased because they are now expected to contribute labor to both coffee production and subsistence activities, because they are producing more gardens, and because men have withdrawn some of their energy from domestic production.

Although the ideological boundaries between the sexes have blurred with development, notions about female pollution and the necessity for the observance of taboos have survived both the presence of Seventh Day Adventist missionaries and the breakup of the men's cult. Pre-contact notions of gender still appear to be used to evaluate the activities and capabilities of women. Many of the activities and roles which were deemed culturally appropriate for women and through which they could achieve adult status have changed little since earlier times. Women's recent involvement in marketing is viewed as a logical extention of their roles in horticulture and animal husbandry. As such, women's primary activities remain linked to the sphere of domestic production.

Younger Women

This category subsumes the life course categories of Young Woman (Yafanae) and Married Woman (Ae). The lives of younger women have not changed radically from pre-contact times. Only a very small number of young girls are sent to the local Community School, and after completion they are expected to settle into village life. Rituals celebrating first menstruation still occur but on a much smaller scale than in the past. The rituals of today are not performed by the women of the 'clan' but by close female relatives of the young girl. Though some girls receive a primary education, in the end, they are expected to settle into village life and marry.

Although young women do not choose their husbands, contemporary parents usually do not force a daughter to marry against her will. Some parents today insist that a potential wife come to the husband's village and work for a few months before a marital arrangement is settled. Parents say this is because some young women do not know how to make a garden and this screening avoids future problems. During the first month of her stay in her husband's village, the bride resides with her mother-in-law. A wedding garden is usually made for the bride. In contemporary Ganaga a couple begins to reside together after the wife's initial month of transition. The *Yafaye* life course category is no longer necessary because cessation of male cult activities means that men no longer marry as a group. These early years of marriage, however, continue to be difficult. Domestic violence is much more common today than it was in pre-contact Ganaga because contemporary couples spend more time in each other's company. Violence also results as people try to maintain the delicate balance between subsistence and income-earning activities.

After their marriages have stabilized young women have less time, opportunity, and resources to commit to extra-domestic activities. Younger women do not have older children to free them from domestic production. Although younger women have various new economic opportunities available to them, most are not able to participate to the same extent as older women. Younger women are less able to convince their husbands to share coffee profits because they have not yet proven themselves. Younger women also do not participate in producer-seller markets to the same extent as older women. The time constraints experienced by younger women mean that they attend market less frequently and earn a smaller income than older women. An earlier study (Dickerson-Putman 1988) found a statistically significant difference in market participation and annual market earnings of younger and older women. Younger women, then, control less cash than older women. As a result they are also less frequently able to join investment-based activities. In sum, the life course position and time constraints experienced by younger women prevent them from taking full advantage of the income-earning opportunities available to them.

Older Women

This category includes the life course categories of Adult (Aloopae) and Old Woman (Litane). The persistence of pre-contact concepts of gender means that older women still experience a discontinuity in their roles at menopause. As such, older women continue to be more positively evaluated, experience a partial role shift to more extra-domestic achieved roles and exert more control over household decisions. Menopause and successful role performance still are prerequisites for the achievement of social adulthood and greater access to extra-domestic roles. Like younger women, older women have also experienced an increase in their work load. This is not a handicap for older women because they simply delegate this extra work to daughters. Older women are also better able to convince their husbands to share coffee earnings because they have demonstrated their commitment to their husbands and their households.

Older women are also able to take advantage of the new income earning opportunities provided by producer-seller markets. In fact, the market earnings of older women can make a substantial contribution to household finances. This also gives older women leverage in household decision-making. Some older women then use their earnings to become involved in women's clubs and investment-based activities. In fact, they often play leadership roles in these new organizations. Younger women become frustrated because they lack the time, freedom, support, and money that afford older women the opportunity to participate in marketing and women's clubs.

The development process has affected traditional relationships among women. This is because older women as a group have lost some of their ability to control the lives of younger women. One traditional role that older women have lost is that of Big-Woman (Gipinae). However, older women still perform important roles as paid curers and midwives.

In contemporary Ganaga old women, as a group, have lost some of their ideological and ritual control over the education and behavior of young women. Today young girls are no longer formally initiated by old women but rather learn about their roles through the observation of their mother's behavior. Old women, as a group, do not participate in the rituals surrounding first menstruation. These ceremonies are now performed by close relatives of the young woman such as a father's sister. Important cultural information is still passed on to a young girl at this occasion. The contemporary use of individual menstrual huts has also diminished the control that old women can exert over young women.

Summary

I have tried to show how both age and gender shaped the roles and opportunities available to women in both pre-contact and contemporary Ganaga. In pre-contact Ganaga younger women's roles were concerned primarily with productive activities. The achievement of the life course category of adult gave older women more decision-making power within their households and access to various socially valued extra-domestic roles. Many of these roles also gave older women the opportunity to control both the education and behavior of younger women. As such, older women were on the top rung of a pre-contact system of age stratification.

The transformation of Ganaga into a peasant community means that all women are now afforded some opportunities in extra-domestic and income-earning activities. While older women have lost some of the control that they traditionally exerted over younger women, various factors allow them to take more advantage of the socially valued income-earning and investment opportunities available in their community. The differential access of older and younger women to these opportunities is now the basis for a new system of age stratification in which older women continue to occupy the top rung.

ACKNOWLEDGEMENTS

I acknowledge with thanks the organizations that made possible the research on which this paper is based. Specifically, funding was provided by the National Science Foundation, the Wenner Gren Foundation for Anthropological Research, the Bryn Mawr College Max Richter Travelling Scholarship and the Sigma Xi Scientific Society. Special thanks to the residents of Ganaga who shared their lives and experiences with me.

NOTE

[1] Information for this article was derived from various techniques including participant-observation, informal observation, key informant interviews, life histories, formal interviews of market women in Ganaga, and a formal economic interview that was given to a random sample of Ganaga households.

REFERENCES

Abu-Lughod, L. 1986 Veiled Sentiments. Berkeley: University of California Press.
Allen, M. 1967 Male Cults and Secret Initiation in Melanesia. Melbourne: Melbourne University Press.
Brown, J. 1982 Cross-Cultural Perspectives on Middle-Aged Women. Current Anthropology 23(2): 143–156.
Brown, J., V. Kerns, and Contributors 1985 In Her Prime: A New View of Middle Aged Women. South Hadley: Bergin and Garvin.
Brown, P. and G. Buchbinder 1976 Introduction. In Man and Woman in the New Guinea Highlands. P. Brown and G. Buchbinder, eds. Pp. 1–15. Washington, D.C.: American

Anthropological Association.

Cool, L., and J. McCabe 1983 The Scheming Hag and the Dear Old Thing. The Anthropology of Aging Women. In Growing Old in Different Societies. J. Sokolovsky, ed. Pp. 56–68. Belmont (CA): Wadsworth.

Counts, D. 1984 Tamporonga: The Big Woman of Kaliai (PNG). In In Her Prime. J. Brown and V. Kerns, eds. Pp. 49–64. South Hadley (MASS): Bergin and Garvey.

Counts, D., and D. Counts 1985 Introduction. In Aging and Its Transformations. D. Counts and D. Counts, eds. Pp. 1–12. Lantham (MASS): University Press of America.

Dickerson-Putman, J. 1986 Finding a Road in the Modern World: The Differential Effects of Culture Change and Development on the Men and Women of an Eastern Highlands Community. Ph.D. Dissertation, Bryn Mawr College.

Dickerson-Putman, J. 1988 Women's Contribution to the Domestic and National Economy of Papua New Guinea. Research in Economic Anthropology 10: 201–222.

Dickerson-Putman, J. 1990 Development or Disillusionment: The Rise and Fall of a Women's Development Organization in the Eastern Highlands Province of Papua New Guinea. Paper prepared for the annual meetings of the American Anthropological Association.

Dickerson-Putman, J. 1993 From Pollution to Empowerment: Women, Age and Power Among the Bena Bena of the Eastern Highlands. Paper prepared for the annual meetings of the Association for Social Anthropology in Oceania.

Faithorn, E. 1976 Women as Persons. In Man and Woman in the New Guinea Highlands. P. Brown and G. Buchbinder, eds. Pp. 86–95. Washington, D.C.: American Anthropological Association.

Feil, D.K. 1978 Women and Men in the Enga Tee. American Ethnologist 5: 263–279.

Finney, B. 1973 Business Development in the Highlands of Papua New Guinea. Pacific Islands Development Program Research Report No. 6. Honolulu: East-West Center.

Foner, N. 1984a Ages in Conflict. New York: Columbia University Press.

Foner, N. 1984b Aging and Social Change. In Age and Anthropological Theory. J. Keith and D. Kertzer, eds. Pp. 195–216. Ithaca: Cornell University Press.

Gelber, M. 1986 Gender and Society in the New Guinea Highlands. Boulder: Westview Press.

Godelier, M. 1982 Social Hierarchies among the Baruya. In Inequalities in the New Guinea Highlands. A. Strathern, ed. Pp. 3–34. Cambridge: Cambridge University Press.

Hays, T.E. and P.H. Hays 1982 Opposition and Complementarity of the Sexes in Ndumbu Initiation. In Rituals of Manhood. G. Herdt, ed. Pp. 201–238. Berkeley: University of California Press.

Josephides, L. 1985 The Production of Inequality. London: Tavistock.

Keesing, R.M. 1982 Introduction. In Rituals of Manhood. G. Herdt, ed. Pp. 1–43. Berkeley: University of California Press.

Keil, D.K. 1974 The Inter-group Economy of the Nekematigi, Eastern Highland District, New Guinea. Ph.D. dissertation, Northwestern.

Keil, D.K. and A. Johannes 1974 Fighting with Illness. Paper presented at the annual meeting of the American Anthropological Association.

Keith, J. 1985 Age in Anthropological Theory. In Handbook of Aging in the Social Sciences. R.H. Binstock and E. Shanas, eds. Pp. 231–263. New York: Van Nostrand Reinhold.

Kerns, V. and J. Brown, eds. 1992 In Her Prime Second Edition. Champaign: University of Illinois Press.

Langness, L.L. 1964a Bena Bena Social Structure. Ph.D. dissertation, University of Washington.

Langness, L.L. 1964b Some Problems in the Conceptualization of Highlands Social Structure. American Anthropologist 64(4): 162–182.

Langness, L.L. 1967 Sexual Antagonism in the New Guinea Highlands: A Bena Bena

Example. Oceania 27: 61–77.

Langness, L.L. 1969 Marriage in the Bena Bena. In Pigs, Pearlshells and Women. R. Glass and M. Meggitt, eds. Pp. 38–55. Englewood Cliffs: Prentice Hall.

Langness, L.L. 1971 Bena Bena Political Organization. In Politics in New Guinea. B. Berndt and P. Lawrence, eds. Pp. 298–316. Perth: University of Western Australia Press.

Langness, L.L. 1974 Ritual, Power and Male Dominance in the New Guinea Highlands. Ethos 2: 189–212.

Lederman, R. 1986 What Gifts Engender. Cambridge: Cambridge University Press.

Meggitt, M. 1964 Male-Female Relationships in the Highlands of Australian New Guinea. American Anthropologist 66(4): 204–224.

Meigs, A. 1976 Male Pregnancy and the Reduction of Sexual Opposition in a New Guinea Highlands Society. Ethnology 15(4): 393–401.

Meigs, A. 1983 Food, Sex and Pollution. New Brunswick, N.J.: Rutgers University Press.

Modjeska, Nicholas 1982 Production and Inequality: Perspectives from Central New Guinea. In Inequality in the New Guinea Highlands. A. Strathern, ed. Pp. 50–108. Cambridge: Cambridge University Press.

Poole, F.J.P. 1981 Transforming Natural Women: Female Ritual Leaders and Gender Ideology among the Bimin-Kuskusmin. In Sexual Meanings. S. Ortner and H. Whitehead, eds. Pp. 116–165. Cambridge: Cambridge University Press.

Schoeffel-Melissea, P. 1987 Woman in Development. Papua New Guinea. Asian Development Bank. Country Briefing Paper.

Sexton, L. 1982 Customary and Corporate Models for Women's Development Organizations. IASER Publication #41. Boroko, Papua New Guinea.

Strathern, A. 1982 Two Waves of African Models in the New Guinea Highlands. In Inequality in New Guinea Highland Societies. A. Strathern, ed. Pp. 35–49. Cambridge: Cambridge University Press.

Strathern, M. 1972 Women in Between. New York: Seminar Press.

Strathern, M. 1987 Dealing with Inequality. Cambridge: Cambridge University Press.

Strathern, M. 1988 The Gender of the Gift. Berkeley: University of California Press.

Young, R. 1974 The Social Hierarchy of the Bena Bena. In Kinship Studies in Papua New Guinea. R. Daniel Shaw, ed. Pp. 137–169. Ukarumpa (PNG): Summer Institute of Linguistics.

VICTORIA K. BURBANK

WOMEN'S INTRA-GENDER RELATIONSHIPS AND 'DISCIPLINARY AGGRESSION' IN AN AUSTRALIAN ABORIGINAL COMMUNITY

ABSTRACT. Based on research conducted in an Aboriginal community in the north of Australia, this paper explores acts of aggression between older and younger women, specifically those in a 'child/caretaker' relationship. An examination of 24 cases of 'disciplinary aggression', most between consanguineally related women, raises the question of whether 'abuse' is really an appropriate label for these acts. In attempting to understand how Aboriginal meanings of relationship and aggression reverberate in women's experiences of their relationships, their aggression, and their victimization, the author argues that aggression in these instances can be interpreted as a kind of nurturance and that hurt is perceived as a potential of women's interaction. The paper concludes with an assessment of the implications of this perception for the construction and experience of women's intergenerational relationships.

Key Words: intergenerational relations, aggression, domestic violence, Australian Aborigines, women's solidarity

INTRODUCTION

"[U]nder what conditions do older women conspire against their younger female kin and even participate in abusing them?", ask the guest editors (Brown and Dickerson-Putman 1991) of this special volume. Focusing on a community in Aboriginal Australia, I present an example of such intra-gender[1] aggression and the circumstance in which this kind of aggression takes place. In this essay, I have three purposes in mind. My first goal is a descriptive one; I wish to add material on women's intra-gender aggression to the ethnographic record. Second, I want to explore acts of aggression between older and younger women, specifically those in a 'child/caretaker' relationship in an attempt to understand how meanings of relationship and meanings of aggression reverberate in women's experiences of both relationship and aggression. In this section I ask if 'abusing' is really an appropriate label for these acts. Finally, I wish to ask what implications these experiences have in the construction and experience of intra-gender relations in this Australian community.

MANGROVE

The buildings that comprise Mangrove[2] are scattered across a half-mile expanse of now mostly leveled sand dunes on the edge of a northern Australia coast. This settlement was established as a mission for local hunting and gathering people by evangelizing Protestants in the early 1950s. By the late 1980s it was no longer under mission control and had become a 'town' with a population that approached 600. After nearly 40 years of mission and government administration, life has clearly changed for the Aboriginal people of Mangrove. They currently live in permanent dwellings, receive paychecks or welfare checks, shop at the local store, take their sick to the local health clinic, and send their children to the English-speaking teachers at the local school. They watch movies on a community movie screen or on their household videos, listen to or play popular music, and attend church services when, and if, they feel like it. But they also hunt and gather the products of land and sea; circumcise their male youths and hold other ceremonies associated with the Dreaming; identify themselves in terms of their traditional countries (tracts of land), clans, and moieties; conceptualize marriage in terms of 'straight' relationships; comport themselves, to varying degrees, in accordance with rules associated with the kin statuses of their Aranda-like terminology; and in myriad other ways maintain an identity and way of life that clearly derives as much from the 40,000 or more years of independent Aboriginal history as from the more recent Westernizing experience.

WOMEN'S INTERGENERATIONAL RELATIONS

Within this community women interact across the generations in several ways: as neighbors, friends, and co-workers. Most conspicuously, however, women's intergenerational relations are kin relations.[3] For example, women interact as grandmother/grandchild, mother/daughter, father's sister/ brother's daughter and mother-in-law/daughter-in-law. In these relationships women can be found working together or working for each other. A woman and her grandmother, for example, might go out into the river's channel to cast their fishing lines together. A mother-in-law might look after her daughter-in-law's child. Sharing can be an important part of these relationships. A needy kinswoman might be given the flour or baking soda or washing powder she requests. Entertainment and companionship may also be an important aspect of these relationships. A daughter might sit with her mother as she cooks the morning meal; a woman and her 'auntie' (father's sister) may visit another household together. Support is also an aspect of these intergenerational relationships; both mothers and their adult daughters, for example, are expected to intervene in the other's aggressive affairs. In theory, attack may also be a facet of all but the mother-in-law relationship; in fact, it is a potential in them all.

WOMEN'S AGGRESSION AT MANGROVE

In contemporary Mangrove acts of verbal and physical aggression are a commonplace of daily interaction. Over the years that I have been visiting this community[4] I have collected material on 793 cases of aggressive behavior.[5] In these cases both men and women attack members of their own sex, members of the opposite sex, and inanimate objects. They also, on occasion, attack no person or thing but publicly express their anger in 'ritualized' form. For example, a man might throw a spear into the air. Or a woman might broadcast her grievances with a verbal tirade to anyone who might hear her as she strides along the dirt road bisecting the settlement.

Women's participation in these aggressive events is notable. In 495 of the cases women are among the initial actors, in 285 they are clearly instigators, and in 147 they are the victims of other women. Women's aggression against each other may be verbal or physical. Here, for example, several women tell me how two sisters fought after one began fighting with the other's husband:

> Woman A: [Two sisters] had a fight and [the elder] got her finger smashed.
> VKB: What were they fighting for?
> Woman A: I don't know. She is at the clinic. They are taking her to [hospital in town about 120 miles to the north]. And that old man [elder sister's husband] was there too. He was trying to stop them and he fainted.
>
> Woman B: Two of [elder sister's] fingers were just hanging [shows index and middle finger]. This one we could fix [shows third finger]. She is going to [hospital] today.
>
> Woman C: They were fighting at dinner time [midday]. [Elder sister and her sister's husband] were pushing each other. Then [elder sister] was hitting drums [probably trash barrels] ... then [elder sister] went after [younger sister]. We heard the sticks only a couple of times and then we saw them holding [the elder sister's] hand and taking her to the hospital.[6]

Women have their own weapons, fighting sticks or *nulla nulla* and many have, like this elder sister, lost or damaged their finger tips in consequence of their battles. In these cases women have also, though rarely, used rocks and knives against each other. In their fights with each other women may also wrestle, pull hair, throw sand, or rip their opponents' clothing.

Women also attack verbally. Here, for example, are my notes on an overheard exchange between a mother and her adult daughter:

> About 6:30 AM. It is just beginning to be light. I am awakened ... by voices. [Three year old girl]: 'Look sugar, tea, and damper [bread]'. Then about one minute later she begins to cry for a cup. I gather that her cousin [a boy also age 3] has the cup (there is a cup shortage). It seems after [girl] cries for about one minute that [her grandmother] takes cup from [boy cousin]. He begins to cry and apparently cup returned to him. [Girl] cries. [Her mother, the grandmother's daughter] begins to talk in a soft conversational tone used by both her and [her mother] throughout: 'You two are not kind to my two children'. [Mother]: 'This little boy doesn't have a mother and father' [Presumably means they are not there at the time]. [Daughter]: 'You hate my two children, you are not kind to them, like you are to children for [my sister and brother]. These two children grew up [in another community]. You better look out, this one's father will kill you with *bardili* [rifle]. He already spent several months in jail. And he will kill you too. He will kill your children with *bardili*'. [Mother]: 'I can't think about *bardili*. You never work for me ... You are always giving me your children to mind when you play cards'. [Daughter]: 'You are always asking me for money, money for tea, and sugar and flour. You are broking me'. [Mother]: 'Well, no good you stay in that house and we argument all day. You go get that house that [a married couple] been leaving. You tell those young boys to find another house. If you stay there we won't be asking you for money all day'. [Daughter]: 'I can't ask those young

boys to go away' ... This seems to be the end of the argument. I go back to sleep.

'DISCIPLINARY AGGRESSION' IN AN AUSTRALIAN COMMUNITY

Children may also be the victims of adult aggression, though this is never supposed to result in their serious harm. My discussion here, however, is restricted to acts of aggression between people who are at least of adult size, if they are not actually social adults.

It is striking that within this community where acts of aggression are such an accepted part of daily life that the severe punishment of young children is neither expected nor tolerated. This is not to say that adults never attack children, for they do. Men and women sometimes hit, yell at, or threaten younger children. Children, however, are usually safeguarded from severe physical aggression. An adult who severely harms a child, can expect to be harmed in turn (see also Berndt 1978). I was told, for example, that:

> If a mother hits the child for something too hard or makes it bleed the father will hit her.

And that:

> If a father hit [a child] too hard, the child's brother, uncle, or [grandfather] would make a big fight and tell the man not to hit hard.

Expectations change, however, as children reach physical maturity. Under certain circumstances, children may be attacked by certain individuals with relative impunity.

Included in the accounts of aggressive interaction between women are 24 that I describe as 'disciplinary aggression'. These are the cases I shall focus on in this paper. The following are examples from my field notes.

March 10, 1978
Woman D: Said she was upset she had been fighting today with [her adolescent daughter] for 'running away'. [Her daughter] threw a stone at [school principal]. Her mother spanked her. 'I was beating her here' [showed behind].

May 18, 1981
Woman E and Child: Last night [adolescent girl] was 'running about'. She came home 'middle night'. Child: She been run off *mangumangu* [elope or go on an illicit sexual adventure] with [an adolescent boy]. Woman E: *Uwai* [yes], for him now [two teenage girls] been fight. [Victim's mother's husband's mother] and [a classificatory FZ] been beltemem now, givit hiding. Before, when mother been here ([girl's] mother and stepfather are now at Borroloola)], mother been killem la *nulla nulla* [woman's fighting stick] for that kind.

August 2, 1988
Woman F: Last night [my daughter] hit [her younger sister] with a crowbar on her leg...
Woman D: [The woman] wanted [her sister] to stop sniffing petrol as she was doing

last night. When she wouldn't stop, she hit her on the leg with a crowbar. Her leg is all swollen up. She was evacuated to [an area hospital].

August 3, 1988
Woman F: [My younger daughter] is back home. She is walking around. Her hip had to be put back (dislocated)?

Women who have spoken to me about aggression at Mangrove do not linguistically differentiate what I have come to call 'disciplinary aggression'; these attacks are usually described with words and phrases like 'growling' or 'fighting' or 'giving' so-and-so 'a hiding'. They are, I think nevertheless seen as somewhat different from other acts of aggression and bear some, but not complete, resemblance to acts that Sansom (1980: 92) has described as "moral violence". I distinguish these acts from others insofar as the target is viewed as a child who has misbehaved, and the aggressor is viewed as a person who is 'responsible' for that child. The victim's apparent acceptance of such 'disciplinary aggression', the absence of interference in the interaction, and the lack of injury suffered by attackers also differentiate these encounters from many other aggressive events at Mangrove. I shall discuss these three characteristics of the interactions in the next section of this paper.

Table I lists the kin term used by an attacker for her target. The reader should observe that although I present separate categories for actual and classificatory kin, the terms do not make these distinctions. It should also be noted that there are more terms than cases because in some instances there was more than one attacker or victim.

These young women were, according to the accounts of participants, observers, or those with knowledge of the event, attacked for a limited number of reasons. Among these, the most common reason was that of premarital sexual behavior, regarded as illegitimate by the adult community (Burbank 1987, 1988). This reason accounts for 58.3% of all the reasons given. The other reasons include the neglect or mistreatment of a child, delinquency, intoxication (that is, sniffing petrol), general misbehavior (like not doing something the victim is expected to do), and breaches of ceremony or ritual etiquette. One teenager, for example, was rebuked because she did not cry, as is customary, when her father died. One woman castigated her daughter for leaving her husband for another man.

Eighteen of the victims of 'disciplinary aggression' were reportedly struck or injured. In only three instances was it clear that a weapon was used in the attack. It may be that the most injury done was in the case in which an adolescent was sent to the hospital after her sister hit her leg with a crowbar. It should be noted that the young girl returned and was walking around Mangrove the next day. Only one aggressor was attacked and not by her target; instead she was attacked by a young woman taking 'partner' with her victim. Neither of these women used a weapon; instead they 'wrestled'.

TABLE I

Relationships of attackers and targets

Attacker calls target:	
Brother's daughter	4
"Brother's Daughter"	3
Daughter	10
"Daughter"	3
Sister	4
"Mother"	1
Grandchild	1
"Grandchild"	1

AN EXPLORATION OF MEANING: RELATIONSHIP AND AGGRESSION

Elsewhere (Burbank in press) I present ethnotheoretical material on aggression as it is spoken of by people at Mangrove. Here, in order to introduce this exploration of meaning, I summarize relevant portions of that presentation. It should be understood that the following represents my interpretation of Aboriginal women's understanding of aggressive action.

Aggression, that is, verbal, physical, and supernatural acts performed with the apparent intention of harming others, have more than one moral valence for people at Mangrove. Aggression can be a violation of the 'Law' – a word used for what is morally right and acceptable; aggression can be a way of 'causing trouble'. Alternatively, aggression can be a means of enforcing the Law; it can be 'punishment' for wrongdoing. Additionally, aggression is seen as an almost inevitable expression of emotion, particularly that which we would understand as 'anger'. Thus people can be expected to aggress in both legitimate and illegitimate contexts.

Rather than protect the community from the dangers aggression can wreak by suppressing it before it appears, people at Mangrove usually provide this protection to one another by attending to manifestations of aggression and intervening when serious danger appears imminent. The public nature of domestic arrangements in this geographically compact and socially integrated community makes such an arrangement possible. Thus when people at Mangrove get angry, it is both expected and accepted that they will act aggressively. It is also expected that other people will pay attention to aggressive events and interfere when necessary.

People do not simply interfere in aggressive acts in order to prevent serious injury. They may also intervene because seeing an attack on someone provokes their own anger. When, however, it is understood that a target deserves the punishment for some violation of expectations or Law, people who might normally fight on their behalf are more willing to stand by. They would, however, take action if the victim were about to be seriously harmed. There is also an expectation that victims, knowing themselves to be in the wrong, will not retaliate, though it is also recognized that even a wrongdoer can be provoked by an attack and expected to fight back.

I argue that it is with something like this understanding of aggression in mind that women attack their younger kinswomen. It is also with something like this understanding of aggression that younger women experience these attacks.

The experience of 'disciplinary aggression' rests not only on understandings of aggression, however. It also rests on understandings of 'relationship'. The importance that perceived relationships may have for actors' experiences in aggressive interactions has been observed by Cook (1992, 1993). In Aboriginal Australia, it has long been apparent that perceptions of relationship constitute a pivotal component of the context in which aggression takes place (e.g., Hiatt 1965; Berndt 1965). Along these same lines, I suggest that the perceived relationship between aggressor and target is a critical determinant of the experience of 'disciplinary aggression'. In particular, the experience of what we might describe as the 'legitimacy' of an attack is affected by perceptions of the relationship between attacker and victim.

Those who attend to and interfere in aggressive events are not usually a random assortment of people. Generally it is 'family', that is, members of a kindred (Burbank 1980; Shapiro 1981) who intervene in aggressive encounters. It is also generally 'family' who administer 'disciplinary aggression'. Should others attack a 'child', they are likely to provoke the anger of family members, regardless of the reason for their aggression. For example, once an Aboriginal man hit a school teacher whom he believed was having an affair with his wife. Before the facts of the fight reached the furthest part of the village, several people assumed the teacher had been struck by a family member of a child who had been beaten in school.

The perceived legitimacy of the attacks represented in these 24 cases is indicated in several ways. Here I infer perception from behavior, or perhaps more precisely, from lack of behavior. It is significant, I think, that in none of these cases was the victim presented as anything other than a target. None of the targets were described as responding to the aggression in any way, though in accounts of other kinds of fights and arguments targeted people were said to fight back. Furthermore, in only one of the 24 cases was it said that anybody assisted a victim of 'disciplinary aggression' and the only reported injury suffered by any of the attackers was that inflicted by this helper. It might also be noted here that this interference occurred in a case where an older sister attacked a younger sibling rather than in a case where an older family member – one more likely to be regarded as a child's 'boss'[7] – was the perpetrator. Lack of participation or response can, of course, mean many things. Elsewhere, for example, people might not interfere in a fight for fear of getting hurt. At Mangrove, however, lack of interference probably indicates one, or possibly both, of two perceptions: that observers do not think the aggression is about to lead to serious harm, or that the attack is a legitimate act. However much such attacks might hurt them, the teenage girls and young women who are attacked by older family members probably understand this aggression as a legitimate response to their violations of expectations or Law.

CONCLUSION: 'DISCIPLINARY AGGRESSION' AND RELATIONSHIP

Perhaps because patrilocal residence preponderates in the societies anthropologists usually study (e.g., Levinson and Malone 1980), our prototype of the abusive relationship between older and younger women is that of the mother-in-law/daughter-in-law dyad (e.g. Brown 1992; cf. Lamphere 1974). In the various treatments of this relationship, women as mothers-in-law are portrayed either as competing with younger women for their only route to political power or economic survival, that is, through their respective sons and husbands (e.g., Collier 1974; Schuster 1985) or as the often abusive allies of men (e.g., Miller 1992; Lateef 1992; Gallin 1992). Let me, therefore, reiterate in this discussion of women's intra-gender aggression that in these cases of 'disciplinary aggression' it is primarily consanguineally related women who may be said to victimize each other. Aggression in these instances can be interpreted as a kind of nurturance. It is critical here to point out that it is precisely because these women are perceived as 'related' that they employ aggression in their interaction. This is not to say that unrelated women never attack each other, for they do. But in these cases it is by virtue of women's relationships, especially those that are seen in some sense as 'caretaking', that they are expected to chastise their younger kin.

In the last decade or so, anthropological treatments of gender and feminism have questioned "the actual, or potential identity between women" (Moore 1988: 10; see also Harris and Young 1981). Of particular relevance for this discussion is Janet Bujra's (1979) dissection of the unitary notion of 'female solidarity'. There is little empirical reason to expect women to act in concert simply because they are women. Nor are we surprised when we find that "women's relations to each other are determined by their relations to men" (Bujra 1979: 33). Others (e.g., Collier 1974; Schuster and Hartz-Karp 1986; Bledsoe 1993) have demonstrated how hostility between women undermines their position in contests for status, power, or economic parity with men. Therefore my conclusion that in attacking their younger female kin, older women are often serving male interests should come as no surprise (see Burbank 1988 for the details of this argument). Here I want to suggest that these experiences of female aggression may affect intra-gender relationships in at least one other way.

I have stated above that however much they might be hurt by the attacks of their elders, adolescent girls probably understand this aggression as a legitimate form of action. According to this formulation 'punishment' would not be experienced as 'abuse'. But I also want to propose that we can, in some instances, have experiences beyond our theories. A physical or psychological attack can hurt no matter how we construct it. Thus I argue that for the women of Mangrove, perceptions of intra-gender relationships between female kin include the experience and/or expectation that women can hurt one another. What remains to be seen is precisely how this hurt affects the construction of women's relationships.

ACKNOWLEDGEMENTS

This paper is based on research supported by the Harry Frank Guggenheim Foundation, the National Institute of Mental Health, the National Science Foundation (Visiting Professorships for Women), and the Australian Institute of Aboriginal and Torres Strait Islander Studies. Thanks are due to Drs. Jeanette Dickerson-Putman and Judith Brown for their helpful readings of an earlier version of this paper.

NOTES

[1] I use 'intra-gender' as an economical way of indicating that I am referring to interactions among women and girls.

[2] This is a pseudonym.

[3] The Aboriginal people of Mangrove address and refer to each other with a series of kin terms. These terms are extended to all known individuals, not just genealogical relatives. Some people, however, are described as 'close' or 'full' relations. Individuals are said to be 'full' relations on the basis of perceived genealogical links (e.g., someone might say, "We are all one mother's mother"), shared clan membership, or a shared "Dreaming" (that is, they are linked by common connections in stories about religious events or figures). It is generally 'close' relations who engage in the kinds of interactions I describe here.

[4] I have visited this community three times, once for eighteen months in 1977 and 1978, once for nine months in 1981, and once for seven months in 1988.

[5] It should be noted that the number of cases is as much a reflection of how Aboriginal people and I conceptualize 'events' as it is of the actual occurrence of those events. Detailed discussions of method are provided in Burbank (1992; in press).

[6] These are generally notes written sometime after a conversation took place. Although I tried to remember and record words verbatim, these notations can only be regarded as approximations of what people said.

[7] This Kriol word is used by people at Mangrove to designate either direction and supervision or authority and control. Mothers and fathers and their siblings are generally regarded as the 'boss' of a child (Burbank 1980).

REFERENCES

Berndt, C. 1978 In Aboriginal Australia. In Learning Non Aggression: The Experience of Non-Literate Societies. A. Montagu, ed. Pp. 144–160. Oxford: Oxford University Press.

Berndt, R. 1965 Law and Order in Aboriginal Australia. In Aboriginal Man in Australia. R. Berndt, ed. Pp. 167–206. London: Angus Robertson.

Bledsoe, C. 1993 The Politics of Polygyny in Mende Education and Child Fosterage Transactions. In Sex and Gender Hierarchies. B. Miller, ed. Pp. 170–192. Cambridge: Cambridge University Press.

Brown, J. 1992 Introduction: Definitions, Assumptions, Themes, and Issues. In Sanctions and Sanctuary: Cultural Perspectives on the Beating of Wives. D. Counts, J. Brown, and J. Campbell, eds. Pp. 1–18. Boulder: Westview Press.

Brown, J. and J. Dickerson-Putman 1991 Proposal for Session for the 1991 AAA Meetings: Coalitions, Conspiracies and Conflict: Intergenerational Relationships among Women in Cross-Cultural Perspective.

Bujra, J. 1979 Introduction: Female Solidarity and the Sexual Division of Labour. In Women United, Women Divided: Comparative Studies of Ten Contemporary Cultures. P. Caplan and J. Bujra, eds. Pp. 13–45. Bloomington: Indiana University Press.

Burbank, V. 1980 Expressions of Anger and Aggression in an Australian Aboriginal Community. Ph.D. dissertation, New Brunswick: Rutgers University.

Burbank, V. 1987 Premarital Sex Norms: Cultural Interpretation in an Australian Aboriginal Community. Ethos 15: 226–234.

Burbank, V. 1988 Aboriginal Adolescence: Maidenhood in an Australian Community. New Brunswick: Rutgers University Press.

Burbank, V. 1992 Sex, Gender, and Difference: Dimensions of Aggression in an Australian Aboriginal Community. Human Nature 3: 251–278.

Burbank, V. in press Fighting Women: Anger and Aggression in Aboriginal Australia. Berkeley: University of California Press.

Collier, J. 1974 Women in Politics. In Woman, Culture and Society. M. Rosaldo and L. Lamphere, eds. Pp. 89–96. Stanford: Stanford University Press.

Cook, K. 1992 Matrifocality and Female Aggression in Margariteno Society. In Of Mice and Women: Aspects of Female Aggression. K. Bjorkqvist and P. Niemela, eds. Pp. 149–162. New York: Academic Press.

Cook, K. 1993 Small Town, Big Hell: An Ethnographic Study of Aggression in a Margariteno Community. Caracas: Fundacion La Salle de Ciencias Naturales, Instituto Caribe de Anthropologia y Sociologia.

Gallin, R. 1992 Wife Abuse in the Context of Development and Change: A Chinese (Taiwanese) Case. In Sanctions and Sanctuary: Cultural Perspectives on the Beating of Wives. D. Counts, J. Brown, and J. Campbell, eds. Pp. 219–227. Boulder: Westview Press.

Harris, O. and K. Young 1981 Engendered Structures: Some Problems in the Analysis of Reproduction. In The Anthropology of Pre-Capitalist Societies. J. Kahn and J. Llohera, eds. Pp. 109–147. London: MacMillan.

Hiatt, L. 1965 Kinship and Conflict: A Study of an Aboriginal Community in Northern Arnhem Land. Canberra: Australian National University Press.

Lamphere, L. 1974 Strategies, Cooperation and Conflict Among Women in Domestic Groups. In Women, Culture and Society. M. Rosaldo and L. Lamphere, eds. Pp. 97–112. Stanford: Stanford University Press.

Lateef, S. 1992 Wife Abuse Among Indo-Fijians. In Sanctions and Sanctuary: Cultural Perspectives on the Beating of Wives. D. Counts, J. Brown, and J. Campbell, eds. Pp. 185–201. Boulder: Westview Press.

Levinson, D. and M. Malone 1980 Toward Explaining Human Culture: A Critical Review of the Findings of Worldwide Cross-Cultural Research. New Haven: HRAF Press.

Miller, B. 1992 Wife-Beating in India: Variation on a Theme. In Sanctions and Sanctuary: Cultural Perspectives on the Beating of Wives. D. Counts, J. Brown, and J. Campbell, eds. Pp. 173–184. Boulder: Westview Press.

Moore, H. 1988 Feminism and Anthropology. Minneapolis: University of Minnesota Press.

Sansom, B. 1980 The Camp at Wallaby Cross: Aboriginal Fringe Dwellers in Darwin. Canberra: Australian Institute of Aboriginal Studies.

Schuster, I. 1985 Female Aggression and Resource Scarcity: A Cross-Cultural Perspective. Unpublished Manuscript.

Schuster, I. and J. Hartz-Karp 1986 Kinder, Kueche, Kibbutz: Women's Aggression and

Status Quo Maintenance in a Small Scale Community. Anthropological Quarterly: Culture and Aggression 59: 191–199.

Shapiro, W. 1981 Miwuyt Marriage: The Cultural Anthropology of Affinity in Northeast Arnhem Land. Philadelphia: Institute for the Study of Human Issues.

MARY S. MCDONALD PAVELKA

THE NONHUMAN PRIMATE PERSPECTIVE:
OLD AGE, KINSHIP AND SOCIAL PARTNERS
IN A MONKEY SOCIETY

ABSTRACT. This paper presents a perspective on the topic of intergenerational relations among nonhuman primate females, reporting on a study of the social manifestations of aging in female Japanese monkeys. Japanese monkeys are representative of many of the well-studied old world monkeys, living in female-bonded societies characterized by the dispersal of natal males. The intergenerational relationships among female kin represent the most fundamental and enduring relationships in the group. The life-time bonds between mothers and daughters are characterized by affiliative behaviors and by mutual support in times of conflict with non-family members. Because kinship bonds persist across the lifecourse, old females do not become socially isolated, nor experience a decrease in social power, nor engage in behavior patterns distinct from those of middle-aged or young adults. Changes in female social networks occur within this strong intergenerational female kinship structure: in youth, a female's primary social bond is with her mother; in old age, it is with her daughter.

Key Words: non-human primates, kinship bonds, aging

INTRODUCTION

This paper presents a perspective on the topic of female nonhuman primate aging and intergenerational relations. Some readers may wonder at the inclusion of a paper on nonhuman primates in a volume devoted to older women in a cross-cultural perspective. The decision of the editors to include such a paper reflects their appreciation of the fact that the comparative orientation provided by a cross-cultural investigation is further enhanced by the cross-species perspective. Indeed, the study of the social manifestations of female aging in just one nonhuman primate group, Japanese monkeys, does reveal some parallels and some contrasts with aspects of aging in human society. Interesting in their own right, Japanese monkeys are characterized by a complex society with behavior organized by some of the same variables familiar to investigators of human societies, namely age, family relationships (kinship), and social power (dominance hierarchies).

With almost 200 species of nonhuman primates, and with great variations in social organization among them, no species can be said to be representative of all nonhuman primates. However because the social structure of Japanese monkeys is characteristic of that of most Old World monkeys – one of the largest and best studied of all nonhuman primate groups – this paper will report on one colony of Japanese monkeys (*Macaca fuscata*). More significantly, the study suggests that some important characteristics of aging in a Japanese monkey troop may be common to all nonhuman primate groups and may represent important distinctions between human and nonhuman primate aging.

Japanese monkeys live in female-bonded groups from which males tend to disperse at puberty and in which females remain throughout their lives. This pattern of male dispersal and female philopatry results in a group comprised of related females normally associated with a number of unrelated immigrant adult males. They are referred to as female-bonded groups because the primary bonds holding the group together are those between related females. Matrilines persist through generations, giving the group its continuity in membership through time.

In a female-bonded group, kinship influences a wide range of behavior patterns (see Fedigan 1992; Gouzoules and Gouzoules 1987). Kinship, as used by primatologists, refers to the relationships among animals biologically related through maternal lines. Since males tend to leave the group at puberty, and to associate infrequently with female relatives if they do not disperse, the primary kinship bond is between mothers and daughters. A female's kin group would include her mother, grandmother, daughters, granddaughters, sisters, nieces, aunts, and so on. The connection between mothers and daughters extends far beyond weaning and the attainment of physical independence, enduring throughout the lives of the animals, and influencing almost all aspects of social life. Close female kin travel, eat, and sleep in proximity to one another; affiliation is expressed among monkeys by social grooming, with kin generally grooming one another far more than they groom nonkin.

In addition to influencing affiliative patterns, kinship largely determines the dominance rank of individual females. Dominance, a form of social power which provides higher ranking animals with priority of access to desired resources, is a complex phenomenon which cannot be attributed solely to characteristics of any one individual. A high level of cooperation characterizes the resolution of conflict situations: in order to win a fight, an individual relies on other animals to provide support in the form of threatening, lunging at, and chasing the opponent. Consequently, the outcome of any dominance interaction or any conflict situation depends heavily upon the social context. Female dominance is both acquired and maintained by the available quality and quantity of support. Herein lies the kinship component of dominance: dominance is determined largely by alliances, and alliances in Japanese macaques are based largely on kinship. Thus, females born into high-ranking families tend to remain high-ranking throughout their lives, relying on long-standing kin-based alliance networks to provide support in situations of conflict. Members of a given family group share adjacent dominance rankings, and whole matrilines rank above and below other matrilines.

Within a given family or matriline, a remarkably consistent pattern has been noted: mothers rank above their daughters, and sisters rank in reverse order of their ages. Mothers always intervene to support and protect infants and juveniles in conflicts with older siblings, and this is the beginning of the dominance relations between the siblings which normally lasts a lifetime. Mothers continue to support the youngest throughout that individual's juvenile life; by adulthood the relationship is set and for the most part accepted by all parties.

I now turn to a description of a study of old female Japanese monkeys which addresses the following questions: What changes would be experienced by females as they move through the adult life course in a society such as this? What are the social manifestations of aging for females in this group? How are female social networks, family relationships and dominance ranking affected by aging? How similar or different is the social experience of aging in this non-human primate society as compared with human society? Does the study of aging in a society such as that of Japanese monkeys serve to highlight any species-wide cross-cultural components of aging for women?

MATERIALS AND METHODS

This study was conducted at the site of the Arashiyama West colony of Japanese macaques in Dilley, Texas. This large intact social group ranging over an area of approximately 40 hectares is provisioned once per day with monkey chow, grain, and occasionally fresh fruit and vegetables. At the time of the study, the colony numbered approximately 400 individuals, which is large for a wild Japanese macaque population but consistent with the size of other provisioned groups.

Focal animal data were collected on a sample of 40 adult females ranging in age from 5 (the age at sexual maturity) to 30 years (approaching the maximum known life span for this species). Animals 20 years of age and older are considered to be aged, corresponding to the third trimester of the life course. Although one individual did live to be 30, the average life expectancy for a female who survives to the third decade is only 23. Few individuals live beyond 23.

Focal animal data collection involves intensive observations of one animal for a specified period of time. In this study the sessions were 30 minutes in length, during which time the subject was followed and its behavior, including all dyadic interactions plus contextual information is recorded, complete with the time of onset and completion of each behavior. These animals were observed for a total of 15 months, covering all annual seasons, between September 1985 and May 1987.

RESULTS AND DISCUSSION

Although the sociology of aging in nonhuman primates is a relatively unstudied topic, the existing literature (often based on short-term observations of small numbers of individual animals whose exact age is unknown) tends to present old age in monkeys as a time of decreased social interaction and increased social isolation (Hauser and Tyrell 1984; Hrdy 1981; Waser 1978; Nakamichi 1984). The first objective of this study was to address the question of sociability and old age: do old female Japanese monkeys experience an increase in social isolation? Two different measures of sociability were obtained for each subject:

first was network size – the total number of other animals with whom the subject was observed to spend time, either sitting in body contact or engaged in social grooming; second was the total amount of time that the animal spent in social contact, again either sitting in body contact or engaged in social grooming. The study revealed no consistent pattern of decreased sociability in aged female Japanese monkeys. No relationship could be found between the animal's age and her score on either of these sociability measures. Neither the social network size nor the social contact time varied relative to the age of the animal, and there was no evidence that the aged animals experienced any disengagement or tendency toward increased social isolation (Pavelka 1991).

In the primatological literature, particularly that with a gerontological perspective, the idea that aged monkeys will be distinguishable from younger adults in their social behavior is prevalent. Some researchers have sought to document the behavioral manifestations of old age in monkeys (e.g., Hauser and Tyrrell 1984; Nakamichi 1984); others make explicit reference to the "aged role" or the "role of aged animals" (e.g., Maxim 1979; Hrdy 1981) in monkey society. Both the term 'aged role' and the assumption that such a role exists are very common. The second question addressed in this study was: do old females exhibit behaviors which distinguish them from other adults? Do they occupy a distinct social role? This line of inquiry looked to specific behaviors other than those addressed under the sociability question. Variation in the frequency and duration of behaviors such as eating, locomoting, mating, fighting, grooming, and sleeping which might correspond to age differences was explored. The results indicated that little behavioral variation within the adult female group was based on old age. Where age-related variation occurred it was better explained as a function of youth than of old age. For example, young females spent more time in the advertising and monitoring stage of courtship behavior than did older females, and this pattern has been reported and explained in previous research as a characteristic of the inexperienced courtship of young Japanese macaque females (McDonald 1985). A moderate positive correlation was found between the age of the animal and the amount of time it spent sleeping or napping during the day, but this corresponded to no change in social behavior (Pavelka 1990).

Role theory in social gerontology focuses upon role-loss and role transformation, and indeed, many social and cultural changes are associated with entry into the latter portion of the lifespan in human society. Aged human females face quantitative and qualitative changes in many areas of their lives: parents become grandparents, wives become widows, employees become retirees, and sometimes the healthy become frail – or more importantly, the independent can become dependent. These statements are simplifications – it is recognized that elderly humans are a far from homogeneous group. Nonetheless, aging in human society has recognizable (albeit variable) behavioral and social concomitants, many of which are addressed in role theory. No role loss or role transition was observed in this study; the life course of these female monkeys was characterized by role continuity from the attainment of adulthood until death.

The absence of a change in the size of the social network or in individual behavior in animals of advanced age does not complete the investigation of possible changes in the identity of a female's social partners. Social networks may vary not only in size, but also in content. If a change in the relationship of the individual to the social group occurs during the aging process, the change may manifest itself in more subtle ways, such as in the content of the social network. The third question, then, addresses possible changes in the identity of the others with whom the aged individual spent time. Both qualitatively and quantitatively the relationship between age and social network (age, rank, kinship) were explored.

The first stage of this analysis considered characteristics of the list of interactants as a whole. Based on the age, rank, and relationship to the subject of each member of the list of social partners, an average age, rank, and relatedness to the subject was calculated. These averages were weighted by the proportion of time that the subject spent with the other individual. The average age, rank, and relatedness of the interactants were tested against the age of the subjects in order to investigate overall changes in the characteristics of a female's social partners at different stages in the life course.

Kinship

Are family members more important at some stages in the life course than in others? Does the content of the social network of a female Japanese macaque change, with regard to the role of kinship, as she moves through the life course? Analysis of the data in this study revealed no correlation between the age of the subject and the extent to which her social partners tended to be kin. The importance of kin as social partners remains constant across the female's lifetime.

Rank

A common theme in human social gerontology is a decline in socioeconomic status for the elderly, with a corresponding reduction in the socioeconomic status of the member of the social network. A decline in social rank with old age has been reported for some nonhuman primates (e.g., Langurs, Hrdy 1981). In this study, the age of the female showed no correlation with the rank of the members of her social network. Like kinship, the overall rank of the social network of a female remains constant across the life course. If a female interacts primarily with high ranking others in youth, she will usually continue to do so in middle and old age. The absence of a relationship between the age of the subject and the rank and kinship of her social partners is consistent with what is known about the way in which kinship and dominance rank are related, as was described in the introduction to this paper. Additional analysis showed that the rank of the social network is positively correlated with the rank of the female herself ($r = 0.78$, $p = 0.03$). Her rank, because it is primarily determined by kinship, is usually constant across the life course. Kinship bonds endure and influence behavior throughout a female's lifetime; therefore, Japanese macaques do not rise or fall in rank as a result of being a certain age or being in a certain age group. Animals born into high ranking families are high ranking in youth and stay high ranking throughout old age. Animals born into low ranking families are low ranking in youth and stay low ranking throughout old age. For the sample of 40 females in this study, age and rank are not correlated ($r = 0.11$, $p = 0.53$).

Age

Age homophyly, the tendency to interact with age-mates at certain points in the lifecourse, has been reported in humans (Hess 1972). This would be true of subadult male monkeys in species in which they typically join a peripheral subgroup made up of males of similar age. But what of adult females? A pattern of age homophyly would show up as a positive correlation between the age of the subject and the average age of the members of her social network. In this analysis, the age of the subject showed a slight negative correlation with the age of the social partners ($r = -0.27$, $p = 0.09$). This suggests a tendency for older females to interact not with old females, but with younger ones, and for younger females to interact with older ones.

The negative correlation between the age of the subject and the age of her social partners was further explored by looking specifically at the identity of the primary social partner of each female – the other animal with whom the subject spent the most time – and the possible age-related patterns in the identity of these partners.

In the total sample, the most common primary partner for any female was her mother or her daughter. This shows a clear age breakdown: old females (20+ years) interact primarily with a daughter; young females (5–10 years) with their mother. It is clear that, when available, daughters are the primary social partner for old females. Seventy two percent of old females interacted first and foremost with a daughter. Likewise, mothers are the primary partner for young females. Ninety percent of young females interacted first and foremost with their mothers. For middle-aged animals (11–19 years), 41.7% interacted primarily with their mothers, and 16.7% with a daughter.

Kinship and age, as important variables in terms of the content of one's social network, may operate quite differently in human and monkey society. For monkeys the importance of maternal kin is high and constant throughout the lifespan, primarily as manifested in the mother-offspring, specifically the mother-daughter, relationship. The mother-daughter age difference leads to a reverse of age homophyly.

Overall, changes in the content of the social network of elderly monkeys are far fewer than in those reported for humans. The identity of the primary partners tends to change from mother, in youth, to a daughter, in old age, and as a function of this there is a negative correlation between the age of the individual and the mean age of the individuals in their social network. This change is a time dependent demographic change, not an age-related one (one that is based on inherent characteristics of the aging individual). No evidence was found that aged individuals withdraw or alter the composition of their social networks as a direct result of an aging phenomenon.

This investigation into the social and behavioral manifestations of aging in the female members of a Japanese monkey troop reveals a continuity from the attainment of adulthood to death which is different from the situation in humans in which the elderly in all societies are socially distinctive in culturally varying ways. To understand this difference it is important to consider at least 3 features of human life directly relevant to the experience of young or middle adulthood as compared to old age, features which are absent in monkey society and possibly in all nonhuman primate society.

Division of Labor

A division of labor is generally considered to be one of the primary diagnostic features of human social life. Leibowitz (1983) points out that underlying any division of labor are production and exchange. Production involves the acquisition of greater amounts of goods than the individual is able to make use of, and exchange occurs when individuals share these goods with one another. Inter-individual dependence is one major ramification of this division of labor. Individuals are not complete and independent subsistence units, but rely on production and exchange for survival.

Humans thus depend upon one another in a direct and fundamental way. The fact of inter-individual dependence is exemplified in the case of individuals who are unable to care for themselves or to reciprocate in the exchange of goods and services. In human society, non-productive members such as children and the ill or infirm can survive because they can depend on other members of the society to continue to exchange with them, even if they cannot fully reciprocate. The concept and reality of dependence are central to social gerontology. Because of the tendency for the elderly to have a higher likelihood of infirmity and because of social norms regarding continued labor in the years when the end of the lifespan is approaching, the elderly are often less economically independent. They may be no longer actively engaged in production. Nonhuman primates, especially monkeys, do not possess a division of labor involving production and exchange. Monkeys do not systematically share food, beyond the nursing of infants. Side by side foraging implies no sharing related to production and exchange. Each individual animal, once weaned, is a complete subsistence unit, not directly dependent for survival on any other individual. Evidence of the carrying of non-productive members in human society appears in the archeological record only recently. Nothing like the care and feeding of incapacitated adult animals has been reported for any nonhuman primate species. Frailty to the point of dependence is not a characteristic of old monkeys because animals in this position simply die. Dependent individuals do not continue as members of the social group. The division of labor and subsequent inter-individual dependence characteristic of humans are absent in the other primates, and this has major ramifications for the social manifestations of aging in human compared to nonhuman primate groups.

Menopause

The lengthy postreproductive lifespan of the human female is unique among the primates. Researchers claim to have found evidence of menopause in some nonhuman primates in the laboratory (see Hodgen, Goodman, O'Connor, and Johnson 1977 for rhesus monkeys). However, in assessing what is offered as evidence of menopause, the distinction must be made between an unusual individual phenomenon, and one which characterizes a population. Certainly, cases of old females monkeys who have ceased to reproduce can be found, but the lengthy postreproductive lifespan of all human females who live out the normal life expectancy is unlike anything that has yet been reported in the nonhuman primates (Pavelka and Fedigan 1991). In Japanese monkeys, the mean age at death for the old females is 23, and the mean age at last birth is 22 (Fedigan 1991). A biological model of the human female life course would show a reproductive/postreproductive demarcation which is quite distinct from the gradual senescence which occurs in the other biological systems (i.e., visual, auditory, cognitive). In nonhuman primates it is not possible to distinguish reproductive senescence from the general biological decline of the organism. Menopause, followed by a lengthy, healthy, population-wide postreproductive lifespan certainly renders the human female life course unique. In social gerontology the impact of nonreproduction on the social experience of aging humans is not explicitly addressed, since it is a universal feature of human life and society, and is generally taken for granted. The importance of this aspect of human aging is highlighted by consideration of aging in nonhuman primates.

Awareness of Mortality

Another fact of human life which has profound implications for the way we approach the end of the lifespan is the *knowledge* that we are approaching the end. We do not have any direct evidence that nonhuman primates have an awareness of their own mortality, and without an awareness of mortality, monkeys cannot be expected to experience aging in the same way as do humans. It is true that monkeys recognize a dead animal as no longer a member of the social group. However, this is not the same as having a sense of one's own mortality, a sense of self, a sense that life is more than oneself. We do not have evidence that monkeys, as individuals or as a group, have the ability to interpret and give meaning to the biological changes which occur with aging, that they think about their own lives as being temporary, or that they contemplate their own mortality. The awareness of mortality may be another distinction between humans and monkeys which must have a direct and profound effect on the social and psychological experience of aging.

CONCLUSIONS

In Japanese monkey society, where females live out their lives in the group to which they were born, the kinship bonds between related females – particularly the intergenerational bonds – explain many of the intragroup social dynamics. Male membership in the group may be temporary, but female membership is permanent. Thus, female lives are structured from birth to death within the framework of the matriline. Matriline membership largely determines the primary social partners of each female, these partners providing affiliation as well as support in situations of conflict.

This paper describes the results of a study into the social manifestation of aging in female Japanese monkeys, a study which identified relatively few changes in female social networks or behavior as they approach the end of their lifespan. The important organizing principles of adult female Japanese monkey society are not age-related ones, and nothing occurs in the later portion of the life course to change this. The gradual biological changes which occur over time in all living organisms are not sufficient to set in motion changes in social behavior, social relationships, or social organization. The mother-offspring bond has long been heralded as the basic unit of primate society, and its importance in youth and endurance into adulthood has received much attention. It is clear from this study that the importance of this primary bond extends to the end of the lifespan, and that the continuity in this fundamental unit of society is probably responsible for the essential continuity in the life course of female monkeys. One change, easily understood in demographic terms, is the switch from the mother as primary social partner in youth, to a daughter as primary social partner in old age. The social support of a female, particularly one who has daughters, is solidified and strengthened with advanced age. There is no decline in social dominance.

Female kinship bonds explain many of the intragroup social dynamics across the lifecourse in the female-bonded Japanese macaque societies, and the results of this study may be generalized to other nonhuman primate species living in female-bonded groups. The situation in non-female-bonded groups would likely be very different. Non-female-bonded groups are ones in which females, and sometimes males and females, disperse from the natal group. For example, chimpanzees are characterized by female dispersal. Females normally disperse from the natal group at puberty and settle for life in the group in which they begin reproducing. As a female chimpanzee ages, she does not normally have any close female kin in the group, but will likely have strong social bonds with her sons, who remain in the group with their mother from birth to death. Mountain gorilla society is characterized by the dispersal of both sexes. Social groups are comprised of unrelated females whose primary bond is to the one adult male silverback (some groups have more than one adult male). One particularly interesting aspect of mountain gorilla society is that females may continue to change groups throughout their lives, leaving behind offspring who have been weaned. Female mountain gorillas apparently do not count on kinship bonds at any point in their lives, making intergenerational relations among kin non-existent. (For more information/references on the social organization of chimpanzees see Nishida and Hiraiwa-Hasegawa 1987 and of gorillas, see Stewart and Harcourt 1987).

The intergenerational relations of female Japanese monkeys which were highlighted by this study of female aging are specific to females living in female-bonded social groups. However, the essential continuity in the lives of females throughout adulthood – the lack of a distinct social role or category for the aged – may be generalized to all nonhuman primates. This assertion is based on the likelihood that the 3 characteristics of human life experience identified in this paper (a division of labor which leads to interindividual dependence, menopause, and awareness of mortality) are indeed unique to humans, and absent in all nonhuman primate societies. Clearly, the subject matter of social gerontology would be radically different if women continued to give birth into their sixties and seventies, if everyone were independent, and if there were no knowledge that one's life would soon, or even eventually, end. Female non-human primates are fully independent (in terms of subsistence) and have babies right up to an end that they probably do not know is coming. The adulthood life course of these animals is therefore more continuous to death, without clear social demarcation of the aged. Of course biological aging does occur, but the social manifestations of these biological changes are apparently not substantial. A model of the human life course, biological or social, will show the aged as an identifiable group, however, blurred the boundary between the aged and non-aged may be.

ACKNOWLEDGEMENTS

Thanks to Linda Marie Fedigan (NSERC #A7723), Lou Griffin, Barbara Smuts, Margo Schulte, Judith K. Brown and Jeanette Dickerson-Putman.

REFERENCES

Fedigan, L. 1992 Primate Paradigms. Chicago: University of Chicago Press.
Fedigan, L. 1991 Life Span and Reproduction in Japanese Macaque Females. In The Monkeys of Arashiyama: 35 Years of Research in Japan and the West. L.M. Fedigan and P. Asquith, eds. Pp. 140–154. Albany: University of New York Press.
Gouzoules, S. and H. Gouzoules 1987 Kinship. In Primate Societies. B. Smuts, D.L. Cheney, R.M. Seyfarth, and T.T. Struhsaker, eds. Pp. 299–305. Chicago: University of Chicago Press.
Hauser, M. and G. Tyrrell 1984 Old Age and Its Behavioral Manifestations: A Study on Two Species of Macaque. Folia Primatologica 43: 24–35.
Hess, B. 1972 Friendship. In Sociology of Age Stratification. M.W. Riley, M. Johnson, and A. Foner, eds. Pp. 357–393. New York: Russell Sage Foundation.
Hodgen, G.D., A.L. Goodman, A. O'Connor, and D.K. Johnson 1977 Menopause in Rhesus Monkeys: Model for Study of Disorders in the Human Climacteric. American

Journal of Obstetrics and Gynecology 127: 581–584.

Hrdy, S.B. 1981 "Nepotists" and "Altruists": The Behavior of Old Females Among Macaques and Langur Monkeys. In Other Ways of Growing Old: Anthropological Perspectives. P.T. Amoss and S. Harrell, eds. Pp. 59–76. Stanford: Stanford University Press.

Leibowitz, L. 1983 Origins of the Sexual Division of Labor. In Women's Nature: Rationalizations of Inequality. M. Lowe and R. Hubbard, eds. Pp. 123–147. New York: Pergamon Press.

Maxim, P.E. 1979 Social Behavior. In Aging in Nonhuman Primates. D.M. Bowden, ed. Pp. 56–70. New York: Van Nostrand Reinhold Co.

McDonald, M. 1985 The Courtship Behavior of Female Japanese Monkeys. The Canadian Review of Physical Anthropology 4(2): 67–75.

Nakamichi, M. 1984 Behavioral Characteristics of Old Female Japanese Monkeys in a Free-Ranging Group. Primates 25(2): 192–203.

Nishida, T. and M. Hiraiwa-Hasegawa 1987 Chimpanzees and Bonobos: Cooperative Relationships Between Males. In Primate Societies. B. Smuts, D.L. Cheney, R.M. Seyfarth, and T.T. Struhsaker, eds. Pp. 299–305. Chicago: University of Chicago Press.

Pavelka, M.S.M. 1990 Do Old Female Monkeys Have a Specified Social Role? Primates 31(3): 363–373.

Pavelka, M.S.M. 1991 Sociability in Old Female Japanese Monkeys: Human versus Nonhuman Primate Aging. American Anthropologist 93: 588–598.

Pavelka, M.S.M. and L.M. Fedigan 1991 Menopause: A Comparative Life History Perspective. Yearbook of Physical Anthropology 34:13–38.

Stewart, K. and A.H. Harcourt 1987 Gorillas: Variation in Female Relationships. In Primate Societies. B. Smuts, D.L. Cheney, R.M. Seyfarth, and T.T. Struhsaker, eds. Pp. 299–305. Chicago: University of Chicago Press.

Waser, P.M. 1978 Postreproductive Survival and Behavior of a Free-Ranging Female Mangabey. Folia Primatologica 29: 142–160.

JUDITH K. BROWN, PERLA SUBBAIAH, AND THERESE SARAH

BEING IN CHARGE: OLDER WOMEN AND THEIR YOUNGER FEMALE KIN

ABSTRACT. Our cross-cultural study of the relationship between older women and their younger female kin examines women's hierarchies based on age and focuses on the exercise of authority by women, when such authority is traditional and accepted. Data were collected for two world-wide samples each consisting of 30 societies, varying in complexity, subsistence base, geographic location, and in customs related to women's lives. Three hypotheses were tested. The findings, which are statistically significant, suggest that the relationships between older women and their younger female kin are patterned and predictable, determined by the role of women in subsistence activities, by rules for post-marital residence, and by descent.

Key Words: women's age hierarchies, older women's authority, women cross-culturally, intergenerational relations

> When domination can only be exercised ... directly, between one person and another, it can not take place overtly and must be disguised under the veil of enchanted relationships, the official model of which is presented by the relations between kinsmen.
>
> The gentle, invisible form of violence, which is never recognized as such .... can not fail to be seen as the most economical mode of domination ...
>
> The system is such that the dominant agents have a vested interest in virtue.
> (Bourdieu 1991: 191, 192, 194)

INTRODUCTION

The preceding articles have provided detailed examinations of women's hierarchies based on age, illustrating the complexity and variety of these relationships in specific societies. In what follows, a more general overview will be presented by means of a quantified, cross-cultural study of 60 societies. Bourdieu's observations, concerning modes of domination, though based on very different data, will be borne out by our findings.

The focus of our inquiry is the actions of mothers-in-law, mothers of married daughters and senior wives in response to certain behaviors of young wives. We are not considering the older women's concern with younger women's courtship behavior, nor with the premarital socialization of adolescent girls.[1] The older woman may be exerting a socializing influence, but typically, the major socializing influences on the young woman have preceded her marriage. In collecting the ethnographic data, we were struck by how readily the behavior of young wives conforms to what is expected of them. Indeed coercive behavior on the part of the older woman toward the young wife is relatively rare cross-culturally (a subject to which we will return), suggesting on the one hand, that girls are effectively socialized before they actually assume their marital role, and suggesting on the other hand, that our conclusions coincide with Bourdieu's analysis of the modes of domination.

Before describing our methodology and presenting the results of our inquiry, it seems appropriate to introduce some of the data from our sample societies. Davis (1983) reports on the all important mother-in-law/daughter-in-law relationship among Moroccan villagers (time period: the late 1960s and early 1970s):

> In her husband's home she [the young wife] must be timid and demure until she establishes herself, which could take several years. ... She must be shy, eyes downcast, and unquestionably do whatever they [her husband and his family] say ... the environment into which she moves is nearly always hostile, due to the presence of her mother-in-law ... The new bride is also expected to take over much of the housework, relieving her new mother-in-law of all duties except the criticism of her daughter-in-law's performance, which she usually relishes (1983:37).

In the following description by Nash (1979; 1990) of the Nagovisi villagers of South Bougainville (time period: the 1960s and early 1970s) on the other hand, the young wife's mother-in-law is not in evidence. This account describes the economic cooperation between mother and adult daughter.

> Mother-daughter relations, on the other hand, are not affected by the marriage of the daughter, insofar as they concern residence and economic co-operation. Economic co-operation is continued, and perhaps even increased ... (1974:40).
> Nagovisi women do not give the impression of being overworked ... they stop at villages en route [to their gardens] to chat and chew betel, and once in the garden, they cook snacks, tend to small children, bathe, and so on (1990:155).

There is contrast here in the amount of work expected of young women and in the atmosphere which surrounds its performance. In addition to being demure and modest, the young Moroccan wife "should not have contact with men outside the family ..." (Davis 1983: 11). Whereas Nash reports for the Nagovisi: "Adultery is common and almost expected" (1990: 164).

THE HYPOTHESES

Are the variations that exist in the relationship between older women and their younger female kin totally arbitrary, or can they be predicted from the presence of other aspects of culture? Our inquiry suggests that there is indeed regularity. When certain forms of post-marital residence and descent are practiced, and when the contribution women make to the subsistence of their society is known, the nature of the relationship between older women and their younger female relatives can be predicted. Of course each individual relationship is also unique and the result of idiosyncratic, psychological factors, but these are beyond the scope of the present study. Our focus is on those characteristics of the relationship which are dictated by the cultural factors we have identified.

ur three hypotheses are as follows:

The First Hypothesis: *In those societies in which the contribution of women to subsistence is minimal, and in which post-marital residence is patrilocal and in which descent is patrilineal, mothers-in-law will confine young wives and monitor their behavior and mothers-in-law will be punitive.*

When women make a major contribution to the subsistence of their society, the work typically consists of gathering or cultivating. (See Brown 1970.) Such female food producing activities make it impossible to restrict the movement of women. However, confinement can be imposed when the subsistence contribution by women is minimal. Furthermore, when post-marital residence dictates that a young wife must live with her mother-in-law, the residential arrangement not only makes possible, but invites the supervision of the daughter-in-law, in order to prevent her from being unfaithful to her husband, from creating a scandal, and from any actions which might be interpreted as compromising family honor. The daughter-in-law is confined to the home; her behavior is monitored. And the restrictive rules may be harshly enforced. But having herself once been a young wife, why does the mother-in-law participate in enforcing the young wife's subordination?

When patrilineal descent assigns children to the lineage of their father, a woman's direct descendants are the children of her son (but not those of her daughter). Assuring the paternal certainty of her son's children takes on special importance for the mother-in-law. Therefore confining her daughter-in-law, supervising her behavior, and punishing her infractions, all are motivated by and become part of the reproductive strategy of the mother-in-law. This is why in certain societies, mothers-in-law, rather than other senior female relatives of the young wife, take on such monitoring and restricting.[2]

Alternatively, if women make a considerable contribution to subsistence, or one that is approximately equal to that made by men, they are unlikely to be confined. If residence is other than patrilocal, the young wife will not live with her mother-in-law, who can not supervise or confine her. And if descent is other than patrilineal, an older woman's descendants include the children of her daughters and sons, which makes the paternal certainty of her son's children less of an issue.

The second and third hypotheses deal with women's work and older women's responsibility for the productive activity of young wives. The older woman may be the mother-in-law, the young wife's mother, or a senior wife. We have limited our inquiry to the older women's concern with young women's productive activities that focus on food: the production of the dietary staple of the society and the food related activities such as processing, preparing and preserving. We also noted the punitiveness of the older woman in response to laziness and uncooperativeness on the part of the young wife.

The contribution of women to subsistence is so extensive in some societies that without their labor, there would be very little to eat. For example, among the traditional !Kung, Lee (1968) reports that the vegetable food gathered by the women provided 60% to 80% of the camp's diet. In other societies, the contribution women make to subsistence is minimal, as among the Rajputs of Khalapur (Minturn and Hitchcock 1966).

Similarly the food related activities of women can be laborious and extensive, as for example the processing of bitter manioc among the traditional Mundurucu (Murphy and Murphy 1974). However to our surprise we found a case where most routine, non-festive food preparation was performed almost entirely by men (Samoa) and another where it is considered so unimportant that it is often assigned to children (Portuguese fishing people).

The role of older women in subsistence activities is independent from their supervisory role in food processing and preparation. For example, among the Havasupai of the southwest, women work to produce the staple food in cooperation with their husbands, but food preparation is carried out within the extended family, under the supervision of the mother-in-law (Smithson 1959). Such arrangements are not arbitrary. Our inquiry suggests that how food related activities are organized can be predicted from the extent of women's contribution to subsistence.

The Second Hypothesis: *In those societies in which women make a major contribution to subsistence, food is produced by women working in groups and typically (but not always) an older woman is in charge.*

The Third Hypothesis has two parts.
Part 1: In societies where women make a minimal contribution to subsistence, food related activities become elaborated and are carried out within the household with an older woman in charge.
Part 2: In societies where women make a major contribution to subsistence, women work autonomously on food related activities or these activities are organized on a community-wide level.

THE SAMPLE

One of the major challenges of cross-cultural research is drawing up a sample of societies for testing the hypotheses. The societies of our sample (see Figures 1 and 2) were selected because 1) their ethnographies contained full descriptions of the data needed to code our antecedent and consequent variables, 2) this sample of societies, although small, was somewhat representative of the societies of the world, and 3) it could be inferred that each society constituted a relatively independent case. The first two criteria are self-explanatory. The third criterion is required to make certain statistical tests possible. Since human societies are notorious for influencing each other, particularly if they are in proximity, this independence of cases is difficult to achieve.[3] A number of samples of relatively independent societies have been drawn up by scholars such as Murdock and his co-workers (Murdock 1967, 1981, 1983; Murdock and

White 1969). These have been used to guide the sample choices for the present study, with some revisions however, in order to include ethnographic sources providing the needed data on the lives of women.

Following the cross-cultural research procedures suggested by Landauer and Whiting (1981), our design required the use of 2 samples. The hypotheses were to be tested on each sample. If the results were confirmed on both, the 2 samples were pooled for the final tests of the hypotheses. Murdock (1967, 1981) divided the world into 6 major culture areas (Sub-Sahara Africa, Circum-Mediterranean, Eastern Eurasia, Island Pacific, North America and South America) and these were divided further into 10 component sub-areas. In each of our 2 samples, every major culture area is represented by 5 societies.[4] These societies have been chosen from different sub-areas identified by Murdock, to insure the relative independence of cases within and between samples 1 and 2. The combined sample consists of 60 relatively independent societies.

Figure 1: Key to the matrix

The ratings have been coded as follows:
The first column gives the identification number of each society.
Column 2 of the matrix concerns the division of labor in subsistence:
   1 = women make the major contribution
   2 = both sexes make approximately equal contributions
   3 = men make the major contribution

Column 3 of the matrix concerns post-marital residence rules:
   1 = all residential arrangements other than patrilocal
   2 = patrilocal residence

Column 4 of the matrix concerns descent defined as the placement of children:
   0 = all arrangements other than patrilineal descent
   1 = patrilineal descent

Consequent variables: column 5 measures the confinement of young wives:
   4 = young women are confined and their mother-in-law is in charge of the confinement.
   3 = restrictions may exist, but the mother-in-law is not in charge; or life in the society is arranged in such a way that women spend their time with women, and men with men (i.e. the "aloofness" pattern in marriage, identified by Whiting and Whiting [1975]).
   2 = young married women are unrestricted in their movements and have the privilege to move about freely (although they may be excluded from an occasional male ceremony).

Column 6 measures the demand for virtuous behavior on the part of young wives:
   3 = mother-in-law in charge of the young wife's comportment
   9 = alternatively someone else may be in charge of the young wife's comporment, such as the husband, or the wife's male relatives
   2 = the comportment of the young wife is not viewed as an issue that needs attention

Column 7 measures the punitiveness with which restrictions are enforced:
   4 = the mother-in-law is very punitive: she beats or starves the young wife, she

instigates the beating of the young woman by someone else such as the husband, she blackens the reputation of the young wife through calumny and gossip or she brings about supernatural punishment.

0 = someone other than the mother-in-law (typically the husband) may apply sanctions, or no sanctions concerning the confinement or the comportment of young wives are reported to apply.

The next two columns deal with older women's concern with the productive activities of young wives. Column 8 in the matrix deals with how the subsistence activities of women are organized.

1 = women work in groups, who is in charge is not reported

2 = an older woman is in charge

9 = other arrangements are reported, e.g. women work autonomously or with their husbands

The next scale, column 9 in the matrix, deals with food related activities, such as food processing and food preparation, food dispensing within the household, food distribution beyond the household and creating stored food. In order to determine which actual tasks constitute subsistence activities, producing food and which constitute food processing, we followed Murdock et al. (1971).

1 = women work autonomously

2 = such work is conducted by the women of a household as a group and an older woman is in charge of the work of younger female kin.

9 = work is organized on a community-wide level.

Because we hope that the existence of our sample will stimulate future quantified cross-cultural research on women's issues, we chose societies in which women's lives range from restricted and limited to societies in which women appear to enjoy considerable autonomy; societies in which women make a major economic contribution to societies in which their economic contribution seems negligible. We chose societies with varying forms of subsistence activities, and societies practicing various forms of descent and post-marital residence. Ethnographies produced during several different periods were used, including several older works which date back to the early decades of this century (Bogoras 1904–1909, Jenks 1905). We have also tried to include some non-American ethnographers (Kloos 1971, La Fontaine 1959). [A full bibliography for the sample societies is too long to be included here. However, such a bibliography is in preparation and will include additional information on the rationale for choosing the societies and their ethnographic sources.]

METHOD

To test the hypotheses cross-culturally, we first defined the variables in such a way that they could be measured, quantified, and scaled. Using these scales, we rated the ethnographic data of our sample of 60 selected societies. Once all the measures had been obtained, the hypothesized relationships among the variables were tested, using the test statistic chi square. The SAS program PROC FREQ is used to analyze the data. (For the sake of brevity, only selected tables will be presented here. The additional tables are available from the first author.)

name	number	subsist	residence	descent	confine	comport	punitive	sub-org	food-org
	C 1	C 2	C 3	C 4	C 5	C 6	C 7	C 8	C 9
Africa									
Bemba	1	1	1	0	3	9	0	2	2
IKung	2	1	1	0	2	9	0	1	1
Mayotte	3	2	1	0	3	9	0	9	9
Nsaw	4	1	2	1	3	9	0	9	1
Plateau Tonga	5	2	2	0	3	9	0	9	2
Circum-Med									
Aritama	6	2	1	0	2	9	0	9	2
Canadian Fish.	7	3	2	0	3	9	0	9	2
Morocco	8	3	2	1	4	3	4	9	2
Sarakatsani	9	3	2	0	3	3	0	9	2
Sudan	1 0	3	1	1	4	3	0	9	2
Eastern Eurasia									
Bengali	1 1	3	2	1	4	3	0	9	2
Iranian Villa.	1 2	3	2	1	4	3	4	9	2
Japanese	1 3	2	2	1	4	3	4	9	2
Sheikhanzai	1 4	2	2	1	3	9	0	2	2
Taiwan	1 5	3	2	1	4	3	4	9	2
Island Pacific									
Alor	1 6	1	2	0	2	2	0	1	1
Hagen	1 7	1	2	1	2	9	0	9	9
Lusi Kaliai	1 8	2	2	1	3	9	0	9	9
Tiwi	1 9	1	1	0	2	2	0	2	2
Truk	2 0	3	1	0	2	2	0	9	2
North America									
Blackfoot	2 1	3	2	0	2	9	0	1	2
Iroquois	2 2	1	1	0	3	2	0	2	1
Navajo	2 3	3	1	0	2	2	0	9	2
Netsilik	2 4	3	2	0	2	2	0	9	1
Tepotzlan	2 5	3	2	1	4	3	4	9	2
South America									
Garifuna	2 6	3	1	0	3	9	0	9	1
Jivaro	2 7	1	1	0	2	2	0	9	2
Mundurucu	2 8	1	1	1	3	9	0	1	1
Sharanahua	2 9	2	1	1	2	9	0	1	2
Yaghan	3 0	2	1	0	3	9	0	1	1

Figure 2 – Sample i

Quantifying the Variables

We examined the ethnographies of a very large number of societies in search of
the quantifiable data we required. On the basis of some pretesting, we created 9
scales, 3 dealing with antecedent variables and 6 dealing with consequent
variables. Each scale at first contained at least 5 possible categories (for the final
analyses, these were eventually collapsed) and each of these 9 scales was
applied to the ethnographies of our sample of 60 societies. Brief definitions for

name	number	subsist	residence	descent	confine	comport	punitive	sub-org	food-org
	C 1	C 2	C 3	C 4	C 5	C 6	C 7	C 8	C 9
Africa									
Aka Pygmies	31	2	2	1	2	2	0	9	1
Bakgalagadi	32	3	2	1	3	3	4	2	2
Gisu	33	2	2	1	2	2	0	9	1
Kpelle	34	1	2	1	2	2	0	1	2
Samia/Abaluyi	35	1	2	1	3	3	0	2	2
Circum-Med									
Al Murrah	36	3	2	1	3	3	4	9	2
N.Somali Herd.	37	1	2	1	2	9	0	9	1
N.Yemeni Vill.	38	3	2	1	4	3	4	9	2
Portugese Fish	39	2	1	0	2	9	0	9	1
Turkish Vill.	40	3	2	1	4	3	0	2	2
Eastern Eurasia									
Chukchee,Rein	41	3	2	0	3	2	4	9	1
Koreans	42	3	2	1	4	3	4	1	2
Malaysian Vill.	43	3	1	0	3	9	0	9	2
Marri Baluch	44	3	2	1	4	3	0	9	1
Rajput/Khalap	45	3	2	1	4	3	4	9	2
Island Pacific									
Bontoc Igorot	46	1	1	0	2	2	0	1	1
Iban	47	1	1	0	2	9	0	9	2
Maori	48	2	2	0	3	9	0	9	2
Nagovisi	49	1	1	0	2	2	0	2	2
Samoa	50	2	1	0	2	2	0	9	2
North America									
Havasupai	51	3	1	1	3	9	0	9	2
Kaska	52	2	1	0	2	9	0	9	1
Ojibwa	53	3	1	0	3	2	0	9	1
Papago	54	3	2	0	3	2	0	2	2
Tlingit	55	3	2	0	2	9	0	9	2
South America									
Maroni R.Carib	56	3	1	0	3	9	0	1	2
Quechua/Inca	57	3	2	0	3	2	0	1	1
Siriono	58	2	1	0	2	2	0	9	1
Yagua	59	3	2	1	2	2	0	9	1
Zinacantan/M	60	3	2	1	4	3	0	9	2

Figure 2 – Sample 2

the columns and for the scoring categories are provided in Figure 1. Figure 2 presents the scores for each of the 60 societies arranged by sample and culture area. (In the tables which follow, headings are presented in an abbreviated form, and the reader can refer to Figures 1 and 2 for fuller information).

In keeping with the usual procedures employed in cross-cultural research, our original plan had been to create scales for only one set of variables, the consequent variables, those dealing with the behavior of older women. In order to avoid a possible halo effect, we had planned to use ratings made by Murdock (1967, 1981) for our antecedent variables. We soon discovered that most of

Murdock's ratings could not be applied. First, many of Murdock's sources were ancient classics of ethnography, written by male ethnographers, and based on information collected from male consultants. Typically these accounts contained very little information concerning the lives of women. Second, numerous recent sources with excellent information on women had been published after Murdock's death and were not part of his samples. Third, a number of other societies included by Murdock had been newly described in recent years and had changed dramatically since the publication of the classic ethnographies on which Murdock's ratings had been based.

Because only very few of Murdock's ratings could be used, almost all the antecedent variables were scored by a 'naive' coder who, at the time, was unfamiliar with the hypotheses, knowing only that the research concerned older and younger women. We made every effort to code all the variables pertaining to one society from one ethnographic source. Where several sources were needed, we were careful to match both the time period of the descriptions and the region within the society being described.

The consequent variables were coded by the first author. Another coder checked the reliability of the scoring for over 20 of the 30 cases in the first sample. Because agreement was very high and so few ratings had to be reconciled, reliability was checked for only 8 of the cases in the second sample. Agreement was again virtually complete.

Scales for the Antecedent Variables

There are 3 antecedent variables and for each, a variety of definitions would be possible. Our choice of definitions was dictated by the hypotheses. The first scale deals with the contribution women make to subsistence. We have not evaluated all the economic contributions that women make nor have we rated the full range of all the subsistence activities of the societies in our sample. Rather we have restricted our ratings to an estimate of the contribution women make to producing the staple food of the society, simply noting whether or not women predominate in the production of that particular food, or if their contribution is roughly equal to that of men.

For the first sample, the 3 groups are not markedly different in size, and show the approximate proportions also found in Murdock's *Ethnographic Atlas* (1967), i.e., societies in which men obtain most of the food are the most numerous, those with relatively even division of labor are least numerous, those in which women make a major contribution are intermediate. In the second sample however, there were proportionately far more societies with male dominated subsistence activities, although the proportions were broadly similar to the first sample (See Table I).

The second scale deals with rules of post-marital residence. This was coded from the point of view of the young bride (See Table II). Where is she living early in her marriage and with whom is she sharing a household? There is consistency in the proportions of the frequencies for each of the categories for

TABLE I
Antecedent variables, column 2, contribution of the sexes to subsistence

Sample 1

	women make major contribution	both sexes about equal	women's contrib. minimal
ratings	1	2	3
frequency	9	8	13
relative frequency	0.30	0.27	0.43

Sample 2

	women make major contribution	both sexes about equal	women's contrib. minimal
ratings	1	2	3
frequency	6	7	17
relative frequency	0.20	0.23	0.57

TABLE II
Antecedent variables, column 3, post-marital residence of the young wife

Sample 1

	all other	patrilocality
ratings	1	2
frequency	14	16
relative frequency	0.47	0.53

Sample 2

	all other	patrilocality
ratings	1	2
frequency	11	19
relative frequency	0.37	0.63

the 2 samples.

The third scale deals with rules of descent, here defined as the assignment of children, as viewed by the women of the society (See Table III). Proportions of the frequencies for the categories for the 2 samples are again very similar.

The 3 antecedent variables are related as follows: subsistence is independent of both residence and descent, whereas descent and residence are not independent, but strongly related (See Table IV).

TABLE III
Antecedent variables, column 4, descent (assignment of children)

Sample 1

ratings	all other 0	patrilineality 1
frequency	17	13
relative frequency	0.57	0.43

Sample 2

ratings	all other 0	patrilineality 1
frequency	15	15
relative frequency	0.50	0.50

TABLE IV
Relationships among the antecedent variables

Sample 1

column 3,	residence		column 4,	descent		column 4,	descent	
col.2 subs.	1	2	col.2 subs.	0	1	col.3 resi.	0	1
1	6	3	1	6	3	1	11	3
2	4	4	2	4	4	2	6	10
3	4	9	3	7	6			

χ^2=2.802; p=0.2464 χ^2=0.553; p=0.7584 χ^2=5.129; p=0.0235
degrees of freedom = 2   degrees of freedom = 2   degrees of freedom = 1

Sample 2

column 3,	residence		column 4,	descent		column 4,	descent	
col.2 subs.	1	2	col.2 subs.	0	1	col.3 resi.	0	1
1	3	3	1	3	3	1	10	1
2	4	3	2	5	2	2	5	14
3	4	13	3	7	10			

χ^2=2.987; p=0.2246 χ^2=1.815; p=0.4035 χ^2=11.627; p=0.0007
degrees of freedom = 2   degrees of freedom = 2   degrees of freedom = 1

Scales for the Consequent Variables

There are 2 sets of consequent variables: first, those that deal with the mother-in-law's responsibilities for the young wife, and second, those that deal with older women's responsibilities regarding the food producing and processing activities of younger female kin. It should be noted that our focus is on the role of the older women and not on the lives of young wives, whose virtuous behavior and hard labor may also be extracted from them by, for example, the punitiveness of the husband or by the fear of gossip. Three scales measure the behavior of the mother-in-law.

The first measures if the mother-in-law is the one to restrict the movements of the young wife, to confine her within the household or the courtyard. Alternatively, someone else, such as the husband, may be in charge of these restrictions. Or young wives may have no restrictions placed on their mobility. The latter circumstances are exemplified by the traditional !Kung (Draper 1975), where young women not only were not restricted within the camp, but also moved around the surrounding territory to gather food. Table V suggests that the 2 samples were amazingly similar in the proportion of cases in each of the categories.

TABLE V
Consequent variables, column 5, confinement

Sample 1

	women unrestricted	other measures	mother-in-law in charge
ratings	2	3	4
frequency	11	12	7
relative frequency	0.37	0.40	0.23

Sample 2

	women unrestricted	other measures	mother-in-law in charge
ratings	2	3	4
frequency	13	11	6
relative frequency	0.43	0.37	0.20

The second scale deals with the mother-in-law's responsibility for the young wife's appropriate, sexually modest, virtuous behavior (excluding industriousness, for which there is a separate scale below). Such behavior may also be enforced by others such as the husband, or the virtuous behavior of wives may not receive much emphasis. The 2 samples differed somewhat in the proportion of cases for each of the categories. Although there is less similarity between the mples for this variable than for confinement, the number of cases in which other-in-law is in charge is consistent. However, these differences between les are not statistically significant (see Table VI).

he third scale deals with the sanctions that are used to enforce the confinement and virtue of the young wife and with the mother-in-law's recognized authority to punish the young wife. Does she have the right to beat or starve her daughter-in-law or to ruin her good name? Alternatively, the young wife's punishment may be at the hands of someone else, such as the husband, or no punishment may be forthcoming. We found punitive behavior on the part of the mother-in-law relatively rare in both our samples. There were only 5 cases in the first sample and only 6 cases in the second sample; a total of only 11 cases in the combined sample of 60 societies.

TABLE VI
Consequent variables, column 6, comportment

Sample 1

	not an issue	mother-in-law in charge	others care
ratings	2	3	9
frequency	7	8	15
relative frequency	0.23	0.27	0.50

Sample 2

	not an issue	mother-in-law in charge	others care
ratings	2	3	9
frequency	11	9	10
relative frequency	0.37	0.30	0.33

The 3 consequent variables dealing with the responsibilities of the mother-in-law are strongly related to each other and these 3 relationships are statistically significant. In each case, the relationships are more statistically significant for sample 1 than for sample 2, but most significant when the two samples are combined. The most statistically significant relationship is between confinement and comportment, when both samples are combined, suggesting that when the mother-in-law is in charge of enforcing a young wife's confinement, she also makes sure that her daughter-in-law's behavior is appropriately modest and restrained. However, the evidence suggests that when a mother-in-law has responsibility for either aspect of her daughter-in-law's life, she is likely to be punitive in enforcing the rules (See Table VII).

The productive behavior of the young wife may be an additional concern of the mother-in-law, but insuring a young wife's contribution may also be the

TABLE VIIA
Relationship between comportment and confinement

Samples 1 and 2 combined

Col. 5 Confinement	Column 6, comportment			
	2 not an issue	9 others care	3 mo-in-law cares	Total
4 mo-in-law enforces	0	0	13	13
3 other measures	5	14	4	23
2 unrestricted	13	11	0	24
Total	18	25	17	60

$\chi^2 = 47.985$; degrees of freedom = 4; $p < 0.0001$.

TABLE VIIB
Relationship between sanctions and confinement

Samples 1 and 2 combined

Col. 5 Confinement	Column 7, sanctions		
	0 not particularly punitive	4 mo-in-law punitive	Total
4 mo-in-law enforces	5	8	13
3 other measures	20	3	23
2 unrestricted	24	0	24
Total	49	11	60

$\chi^2 = 22.026$; degrees of freedom = 2; $p < 0.0001$.

TABLE VIIC
Relationship between sanctions and comportment

Samples 1 and 2 combined

Col. 6 Comportment	Column 7, sanctions		Total
	0 not particularly punitive	4 mo-in-law punitive	
3 mo-in-law in charge	7	10	17
9 others care	25	0	25
2 not an issue	17	1	18
Total	49	11	60

$\chi^2 = 26.190$; degrees of freedom = 2; $p < 0.0001$.

responsibility of the mother who resides with her grown married daughter or of the senior co-wife dealing with a junior wife. As noted above, we have divided productive behavior into 2 areas: first, subsistence activities and second, work that is food related, such as processing, preparation, and preservation.

The next scale notes whether or not women's relative contribution to the production of the society's dietary staple is made by a female work group and if an older woman is in charge of organizing such activities. Alternatively, women may work with their husbands or on their own, or the contribution women make to the food supply may be too negligible to be organized at all. The proportion of cases in each of the categories are similar for both samples (See Table VIII).

TABLE VIII
Consequent variable: column 8, organization of subsistence activities

Sample 1

	women work in gps. no one reported in charge	women work in groups; older woman in charge	other
ratings	1	2	9
frequency	6	4	20
relative frequency	0.20	0.13	0.67

Sample 2

ratings	1	2	9
frequency	5	5	20
relative frequency	0.17	0.17	0.66

Food related activities, such as food processing and food preparation, food dispensing within the household, food distribution beyond the household, and creating stored food are measured on the next scale. We followed Murdock, Ford, Hudson, Kennedy, Simmons, and Whiting (1971) in determining which actual tasks constitute subsistence activities, the production of food, and which constitute food processing. Is organization of food related activities community-wide, with older women in charge? Is the work conducted by a group within the household and is an older woman in charge? Alternatively, does the young wife work autonomously or with her husband? Again the proportion of cases in each category is broadly similar (See Table IX).

TABLE IX
Consequent variable: column 9, organization of food related activities

Sample 1

	women work autonomously or work in groups	women work in household; older woman in charge	other
ratings	1	2	9
frequency	8	19	3
relative frequency	0.27	0.63	0.10

Sample 2

ratings	1	2	9
frequency	12	18	0
relative frequency	0.40	0.60	0.00

No relationship is found between the organization of women's subsistence activities and the organization of women's food related activities. Unlike the 3 consequent variables dealing with the behavior of the mother-in-law, variables which are strongly related, the variables dealing with the role of older women in productive activities are independent of each other (See Table X). This indicates that the organization of women's work in the processing, distributing, and preserving of food is independent of the way women's labor is organized in the procurement of food in subsistence activities. Whether older women are in charge of one type of work can not be predicted from their role in the other. Each area of food-related managerial activity by older women must be considered separately.

Our final scale deals with the punitiveness of the older women in extracting labor from their younger female kin. Is the young woman beaten or starved if she is lazy? Alternatively, the peer group or the husband may be in charge of making the young woman work hard, or there may be no reported sanctions on the lazy, uncooperative behavior of young women. This scale is not represented

TABLE X

Interrelationships of the consequent variables, column 8 and 9

Sample 1				Sample 2				Samples 1 & 2			
column 9, col. 8	food relat.			column 9, col. 8	food relat.			column 9, col. 8	food relat.		
subs.	1	2	9	subs.	1	2	9	subs.	1	2	9
1	4	2	0	1	2	3	0	1	6	5	0
2	1	3	0	2	0	5	0	2	1	8	0
9	3	14	3	9	10	10	0	9	13	24	3

$\chi^2=7.204$; p=0.1255 $\chi^2=4.167$; p=0.1245 $\chi^2=5.895$; p=0.2071

degrees of freedom = 4   degrees of freedom = 2   degrees of freedom = 4

by a column in the matrix, because it turned out not to be a scale at all. In the first sample, in only 3 out of 30 societies was there any instance of older female kin severely punishing young women for their lack of hard work. Milder punishment such as scolding is reported for 3 other societies. In the second sample, there were again only 3 cases of severe punishment and only 4 of lighter forms of punishment. The low frequency of any punishment, but especially the low frequency of severe punishment, in response to lazy and uncooperative behavior by young wives, by elder female relatives is remarkable and a point to which we will return.

TESTING THE HYPOTHESES

When the first hypothesis was tested, patrilocal, patrilineal societies (as here defined) in which women make a minimal contribution to subsistence were indeed found to be those in which 2 or more of the following pertain: the mother-in-law is placed in charge of the young wife's confinement and/or the young wife's comportment and/or the mother-in-law uses punitive measures to enforce compliance. The relationship is statistically significant (See Table XI). (See Feinberg 1980 for details about the tests.) When all 3 consequent variables are present, the relationship is stronger in the first sample than in the second sample, but the relationship is even stronger when both samples are combined. Since the 3 consequent variables are related to a statistically significant extent, the hypothesis was also tested requiring the presence of at least 2 out of 3 consequent variables. Here the relationship was stronger for the second sample than for the first sample, and strongest of all when the 2 samples are combined. The first hypothesis receives strong support from the cross-cultural data, suggesting a robust relationship.

When the second hypothesis is tested, results indicate that the extent of women's contribution to a society's subsistence is strongly related to whether or not women work in groups to produce food, typically with an older woman in

TABLE XI
Test of the first hypothesis

Samples 1 & 2

All consequent variables: confinement, comportment, sanctions, columns 4, 5 and 6

	mo-in-law not in charge & not punitive	mo-in-law in charge & punitive	Total
Antecedents: subsistence, residence, descent			
women's contrib. to subsist. minimal, patrilocal & patrilin.	7	7	14
women do contrib. to subsist., other res. & other descent	45	1	46
Total	52	8	60

$\chi^2 = 21.246$; degrees of freedom = 1; $p < 0.0001$

odds ratio: $\frac{7/7}{45/1} = 0.022$; 95% confidence bounds (0.002, 0.209)

ratio of proportions = $\frac{7/14}{45/46} = 0.511$; 95% confidence bounds (0.302, 0.865)

ratio of proportions = $\frac{7/14}{1/46} = 23.0$; 95% confidence bounds (3.088, 171.325)

TABLE XI: Test of the first hypothesis (continued)

Samples 1 & 2

At least 2 out of 3 consequent variables: confinement, comportment, sanctions

	not present	at least 2 out of 3 present	Total
Antecedents: subsistence, residence, descent			
women's contrib. to subsist. minimal, patrilocal & patrilin.	1	13	14
women do contrib. to subsist., other res. & other descent	44	2	46
Total	45	15	60

$$\chi^2 = 44.845; \text{ degrees of freedom} = 1; p < 0.0001$$

odds ratio: $\dfrac{1/13}{44/2}$ = 0.003;   95% confidence bounds (0.000, 0.042)

ratio of proportions = $\dfrac{1/14}{44/46}$ = 0.075;   95% confidence bounds (0.011, 0.494)

ratio of proportions = $\dfrac{13/14}{2/46}$ = 21.357;   95% confidence bounds (5.464, 83.479)

---

charge. Where women's contribution to subsistence is equal to that of men or where their contribution to subsistence is minimal, they do not work in groups nor is there an older woman in charge. These findings are statistically significant, but not nearly as significant as for the results of the tests of the first hypothesis. The findings for the first sample were more significant than for the second sample. Table XII indicates that the combined sample yields significant results. However, the relationship is stronger in the first sample and in the combined sample when the intermediate rating on subsistence (men and women make an equal contribution) is eliminated and only those societies are included in which one or the other sex predominates in subsistence activities.

The third hypothesis was tested and the results were statistically significant for the first sample, but not for the second. The findings are significant for the combined sample only when the intermediate subsistence category (men and women make an equal contribution) is eliminated. This reduces the sample to those societies in which either men or women predominate in subsistence

TABLE XII
Test of the second hypothesis

Samples 1 & 2

	col. 8=9 all other arrangements	col. 8=1 and 2 older women in charge &/or women work in groups	Total
women make major contrib. to subsist. col. 2=1	5	10	15
women make minimal contrib. to subsist. col. 2=3.	23	7	30
Total	28	17	45

$\chi^2 = 1.988$; degrees of freedom = 1; p = 0.005

odds ratio: $\dfrac{5/10}{23/7}$ = 0.152; 95% confidence bounds (0.039, 0.597)

ratio of proportions = $\dfrac{5/15}{23/30}$ = 0.435; 95% confidence bounds (0.207, 0.913)

ratio of proportions = $\dfrac{10/15}{7/30}$ = 2.857; 95% confidence bounds (1.362, 5.993)

activities. Thus in societies where women make a minimal contribution to subsistence, activities such as food preparation, food processing and food preservation become elaborated and are conducted within the household by groups of women and directed by older women (See Table XIII). On the other hand, where women make a major contribution to food production, their other food related preparation and food processing are conducted autonomously or are organized on a community wide level, both a less confining version of household food preparation. This hypothesis, although receiving some support from the cross-cultural data, yielded results considerably less robust than the other two hypotheses.

CONCLUSION

The findings of this cross-cultural study suggest that the relationships between older women and their younger female kin are patterned and predictable, determined by 1) the role of women in subsistence activities, 2) the residence rules decreeing whether or not older women reside with their daughters-in-law,

TABLE XIII
Test of the third hypothesis

Samples 1 & 2

	col. 9=2 work done in household older woman in charge	col. 9=1 and 9 women work autonomously or community-wide organizat.	Total
women's contrib. is major col.2=1	7	8	15
women's contrib. is minimal col. 2=3	23	7	30
Total	30	15	45

$\chi^2=4.050$; degrees of freedom = 1; p = 0.0442

odds ratio: $\dfrac{7/8}{23/7}$ = 0.266;   95% confidence bounds (0.071, 0.998)

ratio of proportions = $\dfrac{7/15}{23/30}$ = 0.609;   95% confidence bounds (0.342, 1.083)

ratio of proportions = $\dfrac{8/15}{7/30}$ = 2.286;   95% confidence bounds (1.024, 5.102)

and 3) the assignment of children through the reckoning of descent. These factors can explain why in some societies (as Foner [1984] has noted) older women will conspire to keep younger women subordinate.

Furthermore, when women make a major contribution to subsistence, their work tends to be conducted in groups with an older woman in charge. Such organizations have significance beyond the procurement of food. According to a recent cross-cultural study by Levinson (1989), there is less wife-beating in societies that have women's work groups. The opposition between productive labor outside the home and domestic activities, first suggested by Bujra (1979), is borne out by the data here. Household processing of food under the supervision of an older woman is not related to the presence of female work groups performing subsistence activities. Table X indicates that these 2 variables are independent.

In our own society, the managerial potential of older women is under-utilized. The cross-cultural evidence suggests that when their authority is recognized and traditional, older women's managerial style is remarkably benign. Although punitive behavior by older women is not absent, when it does occur, it is more likely and more severe for a young woman's improper comportment than for her laziness. One would logically expect the use of severe sanctions in those societies where women make a major contribution to subsistence, the very societies where survival and well-being depend upon women's procurement of food. However, this is not the case. Possibly the husband or the peer group assume the punitive role. Possibly the young women are well socialized to be industrious before marriage. Possibly the older women's managerial style is so subtle and effective that negative sanctions are simply not needed.

This small, world-wide sample of societies, chosen to vary in complexity and subsistence base, located in different geographic areas, and exemplifying assorted customs regarding women's lives, provides several contrasting patterns in the hierarchical relationship among older and younger female relatives. Older women are clearly in charge. Contrary to expectations, the institutionalized ill-treatment of younger women by their elder female kin is relatively rare, and the few societies in which this occurs can be predicted.

When placed in charge of the productive behavior of young wives, older women administer work that they once themselves performed. Younger women in traditional societies have the assurance of eventually succeeding to the positions of authority held by their elders. There is no glass ceiling; and there are no dead end jobs.

ACKNOWLEDGEMENTS

We are grateful to the Behavioral and Social Research Program of the National Institute on Aging, National Institutes of Health, for making this research possible under Grant 1 R0 1 AG08269–01A2. We thank Barry Winkler for generous counsel, encouragement and support. Our thanks to Sharon Koerber for assisting with the development of the original rating scales, to Michael Burton for advice concerning the analysis of the data, to James Dow for information concerning Murdock's ratings and to Pauline Kolenda for bibliographical suggestions. Many librarians at Oakland University's Kresge Library, Bryn Mawr College's Canaday Library, Harvard University's Tozzer Library and Stanford University's Green Library have helped to make this research possible. Our special thanks to Barbara Somerville of the Kresge Library and to Lynn Schmelz of the Tozzer Library.

NOTES

[1] See for example Broude (1975), Brown (1963, 1978), ana Richards (1956).

[2] This is an unlikely concern for a senior wife. The young wife's mother, on the other hand, may have confined and chaperoned the young woman before marriage, but does not have such responsibilities once a daughter is married. Furthermore, patrilocality might make it difficult if not impossible for a mother to carry out such supervision of her married daughter.

[3] See for example the works of Naroll (1970) on "Galton's Problem".

[4] Burton (1992) also recommends that each of the major culture areas be represented equally, suggesting that Murdock may have over-represented Sub-Sahara Africa and North America in past samples.

REFERENCES

Bogoras, W. 1904–1909 The Chukchee. American Museum of Natural History Memoirs. Jesup North Pacific Expedition (1897–1903). Vol. 11, Nos. 1–3. New York: G. E. Stechert.

Bourdieu, P. 1991 [1972] Outline of a Theory of Practice. Richard Nice, Trans. New York: Cambridge University Press.

Broude, G. J. 1975 Norms of Premarital Sexual Behavior: A Cross-Cultural Study. Ethos 3(3): 381–402.

Brown, J. K. 1963 A Cross-Cultural Study of Female Initiation Rites. American Anthropologist 65: 837–853.

Brown, J. K. 1970 A Note on the Division of Labor by Sex. American Anthropologist 72: 1074–1078.

Brown, J. K. 1978 The Recruitment of a Female Labor Force. Anthropos 73: 41–48.

Bujra, J. M. 1979 Introductory: Female Solidarity and the Sexual Division of Labour. In Women United, Women Divided: Comparative Studies of Ten Contemporary Cultures. Patricia Caplan and Janet M. Bujra, eds. Pp. 13–45. Bloomington, IN: Indiana University Press.

Burton, M. 1992 personal communication.

Davis, S. S. 1983 Patience and Power: Women's Lives in a Moroccan Village. Rochester, VT: Schenkman Books.

Draper, P. 1975 !Kung Women: Contrasts in Sexual Egalitarianism in Foraging and Sedentary Contexts. In Toward an Anthropology of Women. R. Reiter, ed. Pp.77–109. New York: Monthly Review Press.

Feinberg, S. E. 1980 The Analysis of Cross-Classified Categorical Data. Second Edition. Cambridge, MA: M. I. T. Press.

Foner, N. 1984 Ages in Conflict: A Cross-Cultural Perspective on Inequality Between Old and Young. New York: Columbia University Press.

Jenks, A. E. 1905 The Bontoc Igorot. Philippine Island Ethnological Survey. Publication Vol. 1. Manila: Bureau of Public Printing.

Kloos, P. 1971 The Maroni River Caribs of Surinam. Assen, The Netherlands: Van Gorcum.

La Fontaine, J. S. 1959 The Gisu of Uganda. Ethnographic Survey of Africa, East Central Africa, Part X. London: International African Institute.

Landauer T. and J. W. M. Whiting 1981 Correlates and Consequences of Stress in Infancy. In Handbook of Cross-Cultural Human Development. R. H. Munroe, R. L. Munroe, and B. B. Whiting, eds. Pp.355–375. New York: Garland.

Lee, R. B. 1968 What Hunters Do for a Living, or How to Make Out on Scarce Resources. In Man the Hunter. R. B. Lee and I. DeVore, eds. Pp.30–48. Chicago: Aldine.

Levinson, D. 1989 Family Violence in Cross-Cultural Perspective. Newbury Park, CA: Sage.

Minturn, L. and J. T. Hitchcock 1966 The Rajputs of Khalapur, India. New York: John Wiley.

Murdock, G. P. 1967 Ethnographic Atlas. Pittsburgh: University of Pittsburgh Press.

Murdock, G. P. 1981 Atlas of World Cultures. Pittsburgh: University of Pittsburgh Press.

Murdock, G. P. 1983 Outline of World Cultures. Sixth Revised Edition. New Haven: Human Relations Area Files.

Murdock, G. P. and D. R. White 1969 Standard Cross-Cultural Sample. Ethnology 8:329–369.

Murdock, G. P., C. S. Ford, A. E. Hudson, R. Kennedy, L. W. Simmons, and J. W. M. Whiting 1971 Outline of Cultural Materials. Fourth Edition. New Haven, CN: Human Relations Area Files.

Murphy, Y. and R. Murphy 1974 Women of the Forest. New York: Columbia University

Press.

Naroll, R. 1970 Galton's Problem. In A Handbook of Method in Cultural Anthropology. R. Naroll and R. Cohen, eds. Pp.974–989. Garden City, N. Y.: The Natural History Press.

Nash, J. 1974 Matriliny and Modernization: The Nagovisi of South Bougainville. New Guinea Research Bulletin No. 55. Port Moresby: New Guinea Research Unit.

Nash J. 1990 Gender Attributes and Equality: Men's Strength and Women's Talk among the Nagovisi. In Dealing with Inequality: Analysing Gender Relations in Melanesia and Beyond. M. Strathern, ed. Pp.150–173. New York: Cambridge University Press.

Richards, A. 1956 Chisungu: A Girls' Initiation Ceremony among the Bemba of Northern Rhodesia. New York: Grove Press.

Smithson, C. L. 1959 The Havasupai Woman. Anthropological Papers of the University of Utah Department of Anthropology No. 38. HRAF File NT 14.

Whiting, J. W. M. and B. B. Whiting 1975 Aloofness and Intimacy of Husbands and Wives: A Cross-Cultural Study. Ethos 3: 183–207.

JUDITH K. BROWN, THERESE SARAH, AND DENISE PILATO

A BIBLIOGRAPHY FOR THE CROSS-CULTURAL STUDY
OF WOMEN'S LIVES

INTRODUCTION

When a hypothesis is tested cross-culturally, the outcome will be strongly influenced by the choice of societies in the sample of cases used to test the hypothesis. The selection of societies in turn depends on certain qualities of their ethnographic accounts. The bibliography that follows lists the sources that were consulted for each of the societies that made up the sample used to test the hypotheses in the previous chapter.

This sample, like any other cross-cultural samples, is not entirely random, because the selected societies have to meet certain criteria. First, their ethnographies must contain the full information needed to code the antecedent and consequent variables specified in the hypothesis to be tested. Second, the sample is always only a small selection of all human societies, yet it must be sufficiently representative to allow for generalizations concerning humanity as a whole. Third, each society in the sample must constitute a relatively independent case. The first two criteria are self-explanatory. The third criterion is required for the statistical tests of significance. Since human societies are notorious for influencing each other, particularly if they are in proximity, this independence of cases is difficult to achieve.

Meeting these criteria can be facilitated by simply using published samples created by, among others, Murdock (e.g., Murdock 1967, 1981, 1983; Murdock and White 1969) and more recently by Burton, Moore, Whiting, and Romney (1996), thus avoiding the laborious procedures for drawing up a sample. Murdock (1967, 1981) divides the world into six major culture areas based in part on geography (Sub-Sahara Africa, Circum-Mediterranean, Eastern Eurasia, Island Pacific, North America, and South America), and these are each divided into ten sub-areas. More recently, Burton et al. (1996) identify nine regions of the world, based on aspects of social structure. Burton et al. do not identify sub-areas. In using the published samples, one can more readily satisfy the second criterion (representativeness) as well as the third criterion (the relative independence of cases) by selecting societies from different major culture areas and, when using Murdock's samples, from the different sub-areas.

However, if the published samples are used, the first criterion (fullness of ethnographic information) presents a special problem when testing hypotheses dealing with women's issues. Here the samples drawn up by Murdock can be used only as preliminary guides because most of the ethnographies for these societies are written by men and based on information provided largely by male consultants. To apply a cross-cultural test to hypotheses dealing with women's issues, as was done in the previous chapter, a new sample had to be created, one consisting of societies whose ethnographies provide full information on the lives of women. In addition to meeting the three criteria noted above, this new cross-cultural sample was drawn up to contain societies that (1) range from those in which the lives of women are severely restricted (for example, societies in which *purdah* is practiced) to those in which women appear to enjoy considerable autonomy; (2) range from those in which women make a major economic contribution (as defined in the previous chapter) to those in which their economic contribution is negligible; (3) vary in their physical setting and depend on different types of subsistence activities; and (4) practice various forms of descent and post-marital residence. To avoid possible biases in the data, ethnographies produced during several different epochs were used, including several older sources as well as recent ones. An attempt was made to include the works of male and female ethnographers and some non-American anthropologists.

Certain portions of the sample were easier to assemble than others. For example, it was difficult to find a sufficient number of full accounts of the lives of women in fishing and in herding societies. Turkey and Korea presented particular difficulties because the needed information was scattered over many sources. Ideally, a single descriptive account should be used for creating all the ratings for a particular society because all the variables for that society are then rated for the same location and for the same time period. However, in most cases, several ethnographies had to be consulted to produce the scores reported in the previous chapter. Care was taken that all sources were contemporaneous and dealt with the same region.

Following the cross-cultural research procedures suggested by Landauer and Whiting (1981), two world-wide samples were used to test the hypotheses in the previous chapter. The cases in each sample were assumed to be relatively independent, since they were selected from different sub-areas identified by Murdock. The societies of each of the two samples were also chosen to be independent of each other, so that the samples could be combined and still consist of independent cases. The hypotheses were first tested on each sub-sample. When the results were confirmed on both, the two samples were then pooled for the final tests of the hypotheses. This provided three tests for the hypotheses and rendered more robust findings.

What follows after the reference list for this introductory material is not an alphabetized list of publications. Rather, a separate bibliography for each sub-sample is provided so that scholars can use them separately or in combination. Within each of the two samples, the six major culture areas are identified. Their component five societies (drawn from different sub-areas) are named, and their ethnographic sources are listed by author in alphabetical order.

It is hoped that the bibliography, and the sample of societies to which it refers, will provide a stimulus for future quantified cross-cultural research on women's issues. New ethnographies with richly detailed descriptions of the worlds of women continue to be published. It is therefore also hoped that different and larger samples will be developed in the future, making it possible to test more hypotheses and thus furthering our knowledge about women's lives.

REFERENCES

Burton, M., C. Moore, J.W.M. Whiting, and A.K. Romney 1996 Regions Based on Social Structure. Current Anthropology 37(1): 87–123.

Landauer, T.K. and J.W.M. Whiting 1981 Correlates and Consequences of Stress in Infancy. In Handbook of Cross-Cultural Human Development. R.H. Munroe, R.L. Munroe, and B.B. Whiting, eds. Pp. 355–375. New York: Garland.

Murdock, G.P. 1967 Ethnographic Atlas. Pittsburgh: University of Pittsburgh Press.

Murdock, G.P. 1981 Atlas of World Cultures. Pittsburgh: University of Pittsburgh Press.

Murdock, G.P. 1983 Outline of World Cultures. Sixth rev. ed. New Haven, CT: Human Relations Area Files Press.

Murdock, G.P. and D.R. White 1969 Standard Cross-Cultural Sample. Ethnology 8: 329–369.

BIBLIOGRAPHY FOR SAMPLE 1

AFRICA

Bemba

Richards, A. 1956 Chisungu: A Girls' Initiation Ceremony among the Bemba of Northern Rhodesia. New York: Grove Press.

Richards, A. 1961 [1939] Land, Labour and Diet in Northern Rhodesia. New York: Oxford University Press.

Richards, A. 1974 The 'Position' of Women: An Anthropological View. Cambridge Anthropology 1(3): 3–10.

!Kung

Draper, P. 1975 !Kung Women: Contrasts in Sexual Egalitarianism in Foraging and Sedentary Contexts. In Toward an Anthropology of Women. R. Reiter, ed. Pp. 77–109. New York: Monthly Review Press.

Lee, R.B. 1968 What Hunters Do For a Living, or, How to Make Out on Scarce Resources. In Man the Hunter. R. Lee and I. DeVore, eds. Pp. 30–48. Chicago: Aldine.

Lee, R.B. 1979 The !Kung San: Men, Women, and Work in a Foraging Society. New York: Cambridge University Press.

Lee, R.B. 1984 The Dobe !Kung. New York: Holt, Rinehart and Winston.

Lee, R.B. 1992 Work, Sexuality, and Aging among !Kung Women. In In Her Prime: New Views of Middle-Aged Women. Second edition. V. Kerns and J.K. Brown, eds. Pp. 35–46. Urbana: University of Illinois Press.

Marshall, L. 1976 The !Kung of Nyae Nyae. Cambridge, MA: Harvard University Press.

Mayotte

Lambek, M. 1981 Human Spirits: A Cultural Account of Trance in Mayotte. New York: Cambridge University Press.

Lambek, M. 1985 Motherhood and Other Careers in Mayotte (Comoro Islands). In In Her Prime: New Views of Middle-Aged Women. Second edition. V. Kerns and J.K. Brown, eds. Pp. 77–92. Urbana: University of Illinois Press.

Nsaw (Nso)

Kaberry, P.M. 1952 Women of the Grassfields. London: Her Majesty's Stationery Office.

Plateau Tonga

Colson, E. 1958 Marriage and the Family among the Plateau Tonga of Northern Rhodesia. Manchester, England: Manchester University Press.
Colson, E. 1961 Plateau Tonga. In Matrilineal Kinship. D. Schneider and K. Gough, eds. Pp. 36–95. Berkeley and Los Angeles: University of California Press.
Colson, E. 1962 The Plateau Tonga of Northern Rhodesia (Zambia): Social and Religious Studies. Manchester, England: Manchester University Press.

CIRCUM-MEDITERRANEAN

Aritama (Columbian Mestizo)

Reichel-Dolmatoff, G. and A. Reichel-Dolmatoff 1961 The People of Aritama. Chicago: University of Chicago Press.

Newfoundland Maritime Villagers

Davis, D.L. 1983 Blood and Nerves: An Ethnographic Focus on Menopause. Social and Economic Studies No. 28. St. John's, Newfoundland: Institute of Social and Economic Research of Memorial University of Newfoundland.

Morocco

Bowen, D.L. 1985 Women and Public Health in Morocco: One Family's Experience. In Women and the Family in the Middle East: New Voices of Change. E.W. Fernea, ed. Pp. 134–144. Austin: University of Texas Press.
Davis, S.S. 1983 Patience and Power: Women's Lives in a Moroccan Village. Cambridge, MA: Schenkman.
Davis, S. and D. Davis 1989 Adolescence in a Moroccan Town: Making Social Sense. New Brunswick, NJ: Rutgers University Press.
Dwyer, D.H. 1978 Images and Self-Images: Male and Female in Morocco. New York: Columbia University Press.
Maher, V. 1978 Women and Social Change in Morocco. In Women in the Muslim World. L. Beck and N. Keddie, eds. Pp. 100–123. Cambridge, MA: Harvard University Press.
Mernissi, F. 1975 Beyond the Veil: Male-Female Dynamics in a Modern Muslim Society. Cambridge, MA: Schenkman.

Muhammad, Z. 1977 A Rural Woman of Morocco. In Middle Eastern Muslim Women Speak. E.W. Fernea and B.Q. Bezirgan, eds. Pp. 201–217. Austin: University of Texas Press.

Rosen, L. 1978 The Negotiation of Reality: Male-Female Relations in Sefrou, Morocco. In Women in the Muslim World. L. Beck and N. Keddie, eds. Pp. 561–584. Cambridge, MA: Harvard University Press.

Sarakatsani (Greek)

Campbell, J.K. 1964 Honour, Family and Patronage. New York: Oxford University Press.

Campbell, J.K. 1966 Honour and the Devil. In Honor and Shame: The Values of Mediterranean Society. J. Peristiany, ed. Pp. 139–170. Chicago: University of Chicago Press.

Sudan (Villagers)

Boddy, J. 1985 Bucking the Agnatic System: Status and Strategies in Rural Northern Sudan. In In Her Prime: New Views of Middle-Aged Women. Second edition. V. Kerns and J.K. Brown, eds. Pp. 141–153. Urbana: University of Illinois Press.

Boddy, J. 1989 Wombs and Alien Spirits: Women, Men, and the Zar Cult in Northern Sudan. Madison: University of Wisconsin Press.

Fluehr-Lobban, C. 1977 Agitation for Change in the Sudan. In Sexual Stratification: A Cross-Cultural View. A. Schlegel, ed. Pp. 127–143. New York: Columbia University Press.

EASTERN EURASIA

Bengali

Bertocci, P. 1992 Bengali. In Encyclopedia of World Cultures. Vol. 3, South Asia. P. Hockings, ed. Pp. 29–35. Boston: G.K. Hall.

Feldman, S. and F.E. McCarthy 1981 Conditions Influencing Rural and Town Women's Participation in the Labor Force. In Women, Politics, and Literature in Bengal. C.B. Seely, ed. Pp. 19–30. East Lansing: Asian Studies Center, Michigan State University.

Roy, M. 1972 Bengali Women. Chicago: University of Chicago Press.

Iranian Villagers

Friedl, E. 1983 State Ideology and Village Women. In Women and Revolution in Iran. G. Nashat, ed. Pp. 217–230. Boulder: Westview Press.

Friedl, E. 1989 Lives in an Iranian Village: Women of Deh Koh. Washington, DC: Smithsonian Institution Press.

Hegland, M.E. 1983 Aliabad Women: Revolution as Religious Activity. In Women and Revolution in Iran. G. Nashat, ed. Pp. 171–194. Boulder: Westview Press.

Hegland, M.E. 1992 Wife Abuse and the Political System: A Middle Eastern Case. In Sanctions and Sanctuary: Cultural Perspectives on the Beating of Wives. D. Counts, J.K. Brown, and J. Campbell, eds. Pp. 203–218. Boulder: Westview Press.

Mahdavi, S. 1985 The Position of Women in Shi'a Iran: Views of the 'Ulama'. In Women and the Family in the Middle East. E.W. Fernea, ed. Pp. 255–268. Austin: University of Texas Press.

Nashat, G. 1983 Women in the Ideology of the Islamic Republic. In Women and Revolution in Iran. G. Nashat, ed. Pp. 195–216. Boulder: Westview Press.

Japan

Bernstein, G.L. 1976 Women in Rural Japan. In Women in Changing Japan. J. Lebra, J. Paulson, and E. Powers, eds. Pp. 25–49. Boulder: Westview Press.

Bernstein, G.L. 1983 Haruko's World: A Japanese Farm Woman and Her Community. Stanford: Stanford University Press.

De Vos, G. 1973 Socialization for Achievement: Essays on the Cultural Psychology of the Japanese. Berkeley and Los Angeles: University of California Press.

Dore, R. 1978 Shinohata: A Portrait of a Japanese Village. London: Allen Lane.

Lebra, T.S. 1984 Japanese Women: Constraint and Fulfillment. Honolulu: University of Hawaii Press.

Nakane, C. 1967 Kinship and Economic Organization in Rural Japan. New York: Humanities Press.

Smith, R.J. and E.L. Wiswell 1982 The Women of Suye Mura. Chicago: University of Chicago Press.

Sheikhanzai

Tavakolian, B. 1984 Women and Socioeconomic Change among Sheikhanzai Nomads of Western Afghanistan. Middle East Journal 38(3): 433–453.

Tavakolian, B. 1987 Sheikhanzai Women: Sisters, Mothers, and Wives. Ethnos 52: 180–199.

Taiwan

Davin, D. 1975 Women in the Countryside of China. In Women in Chinese Society. M. Wolf and R. Witke, eds. Pp. 243–273. Stanford: Stanford University Press.

Gallin, R. 1992 Wife Abuse in the Context of Development and Change: A Chinese (Taiwanese) Case. In Sanctions and Sanctuary: Cultural Perspectives on the Beating of Wives. D.A. Counts, J.K. Brown, and J.C. Campbell, eds. Pp. 219–227. Boulder: Westview Press.

Wolf, M. 1968 The House of Lim. New York: Appleton-Century-Crofts.

Wolf, M. 1972 Women and the Family in Rural Taiwan. Stanford: Stanford University Press.

Wolf, M. 1974 Chinese Women: Old Skills in a New Context. In Women, Culture, and Society. M. Rosaldo and L. Lamphere, eds. Pp. 157–172. Stanford: Stanford University Press.

Wolf, M. 1975 Women and Suicide in China. In Women in Chinese Society. M. Wolf and R. Witke, eds. Pp. 111–141. Stanford: Stanford University Press.

ISLAND PACIFIC

Alor

DuBois, C. 1940 How They Pay Debts in Alor. Asia 40: 482–486.

DuBois, C. 1960 [1944] The People of Alor: A Social-Psychological Study of an East Indian Island. Cambridge, MA: Harvard University Press.

Hagen—Melpa

Josiphedes, L. 1982 Suppressed and Overt Antagonism: A Study in Aspects of Power and Reciprocity among the Northern Melpa. Research in Melanesia Occasional Paper No. 2. Port Morseby: University of Papua New Guinea.

Strathern, A. and M. Strathern 1969 Marriage in Melpa. In Pigs, Pearshells, and Women: Marriage in the New Guinea Highlands. R.M. Glasse and M.J. Meggitt, eds. Pp. 138-158. Englewood Cliffs, NJ: Prentice Hall.

Strathern, M. 1972 Women in Between. New York: Seminar Press.

Strathern, M. 1981 Self-interest and the Social Good: Some Implications of Hagen Gender Imagery. In Sexual Meanings. S. Ornter and H. Whitehead, eds. Pp. 166–191. New York: Cambridge University Press.

Lusi Kaliai

Counts, D.A. 1980 Fighting Back Is Not the Way: Suicide and the Women of Kaliai. American Ethnologist 7(2): 332–351.

Counts, D.A. 1985 Tamparonga: "The Big Women" of Kaliai (Papua New Guinea). In In Her Prime: New Views of Middle-Aged Women. Second edition. V. Kerns and J.K. Brown, eds. Pp. 61–74. Urbana: University of Illinois Press.

Counts, D.A. 1990 Beaten Wife, Suicidal Woman: Domestic Violence in Kaliai, West New Britain. Pacific Studies 13(3): 151–169.

Tiwi

Goodale, J.C. 1974 Tiwi Wives: A Study of the Women of Melville Island, North Australia. Seattle: University of Washington Press.

Hart, C.W.M. and A. Pilling 1960 The Tiwi of North Australia. New York: Holt, Rinehart and Winston.

Hart, C.W.M., A. Pilling, and J.C. Goodale 1988 The Tiwi of North Australia. Third edition. New York: Holt, Rinehart and Winston.

Truk

Gladwin, T. and S.B. Sarason 1953 Truk: Man in Paradise. Viking Fund Publications in Anthropology No. 20. New York: Wenner-Gren Foundation for Anthropological Research.

Goodenough, W. 1978 [1951] Property, Kin, and Community on Truk. Hamden, CT: Archon Books.

Schneider, D.M. 1961 Truk. In Matrilineal Kinship. D.M. Schneider and K. Gough, eds. Pp. 202–233. Berkeley and Los Angeles: University of California Press.

Swartz, M.J. 1958 Sexuality and Aggression in Romonum, Truk. American Anthropologist 60: 467–486.

NORTH AMERICA

Blackfoot—Piegan-Blood

Lewis, O. 1970 [1943] Manly-Hearted Women among the Northern Piegan. In Anthropological Essays. Pp. 213–228. New York: Random House.

McFee, M. 1972 Modern Blackfeet: Montanans on a Reservation. New York: Holt, Rinehart and Winston.

Price, J. 1988 [1979] Indians of Canada: Cultural Dynamics. Salem, WI: Sheffield Publishing Co.

Wissler, C. 1911 The Social Life of the Blackfoot Indians. Anthropological Papers of the American Museum of Natural History, Vol. 7, No. 1. New York: American Museum of Natural History.

Iroquois

Brown, J.K. 1970 Economic Organization and the Position of Women among the Iroquois. Ethnohistory 17(3–4): 151–167.

Parker, A.C. 1968 [1910] Iroquois Uses of Maize and Other Food Plants. In Parker on the Iroquois. W.N. Fenton, ed. Pp. 1–119. Syracuse, NY: Syracuse University Press.

Seaver, J. 1961 [1824] A Narrative of the Life of Mrs. Mary Jemison. New York: Corinth Books.

Wallace, A.F.C. 1978 Origins of the Longhouse Religion. In Handbook of North American Indians. Vol. 15, Northeast. B. Trigger, ed. Pp. 442–448. Washington, DC: Smithsonian Institution.

Navajo

Aberle, D. 1961 Navaho [*sic*]. In Matrilineal Kinship. D. Schneider and K. Gough, eds. Pp. 96–201. Berkeley and Los Angeles: University of California Press.

Downs, J. 1972 The Navajo. New York: Holt, Rinehart and Winston.

Leighton, D. and C. Kluckhohn 1947 Children of the People. Cambridge, MA: Harvard University Press.

Netsilik

Balikci, A. 1970 The Netsilik Eskimo. New York: Natural History Press.

Boas, F. 1964 [1888] The Central Eskimo. Lincoln: University of Nebraska Press.

Tepoztlan

Lewis, O. 1951 Life in a Mexican Village: Tepoztlan Restudied. Urbana: University of Illinois Press.

Lewis, O. 1960 Tepoztlan: Village in Mexico. New York: Holt, Rinehart and Winston.

SOUTH AMERICA

Garífuna

Kerns, V. 1983 Women and the Ancestors: Black Carib Kinship and Ritual. Urbana: University of Illinois Press.

Kerns, V. 1992 Female Control of Sexuality: Garífuna Women at Middle Age. In In Her Prime: New Views of Middle-Aged Women. Second edition. V. Kerns and J.K. Brown, eds. Pp. 95–111. Urbana: University of Illinois Press.

Jivaro

Harner, M.J. 1973 The Jivaro: People of the Sacred Waterfalls. Garden City, NY: Doubleday Anchor.

Mundurucù

Murphy, R.F. 1973 Social Structure and Sex Antagonism. In Peoples and Cultures of Native South America. D. Gross, ed. Pp. 213–224. New York: Natural History Press.

Murphy, Y. and R.F. Murphy 1974 Women of the Forest. New York: Columbia University Press.

Sharanahua

Siskind, J. 1973 To Hunt in the Morning. New York: Oxford University Press.

Yaghan

Gusinde, M. 1961 [1937]. The Yamana: The Life and Thought of the Water Nomads of Cape Horn. F. Schuetze, trans. New Haven, CT: Human Relations Area Files Press.

BIBLIOGRAPHY FOR SAMPLE 2

AFRICA

Aka Pygmies

Hewlett, B. 1991 Intimate Fathers: The Nature and Context of Aka Pygmy Paternal Infant Care. Ann Arbor: University of Michigan Press.

Hewlett, B. 1992 Husband-Wife Reciprocity and the Father-Infant Relationship among Aka Pygmies. In Father-Child Relations: Cultural and Biosocial Contexts. B. Hewlett, ed. Pp. 153–176. New York: Aldine de Gruyter.

Bakgalagadi

Solway, J. 1981 Women, Marriage, and the Domestic Cycle in Bakgalagadi Society. Paper presented at the meetings of the Canadian Ethnology Society, Ottawa.

Solway, J. 1990 Affines and Spouses, Friends and Lovers: The Passing of Polygyny in Botswana. Journal of Anthropological Research 46(1): 41–66.

Solway, J. 1992 Middle-Aged Women in Bakgalagadi Society (Botswana). In In Her Prime: New Views of Middle-Aged Women. Second edition. V. Kerns and J.K. Brown, eds. Pp. 49–58. Urbana: University of Illinois Press.

Gisu

Heald, S. 1989 Controlling Anger: The Sociology of Gisu Violence. New York: St. Martin's Press.

La Fontaine, J.S. 1959 The Gisu of Uganda. Ethnographic Survey of Africa, East Central Africa, Part 10. London: International African Institute.

La Fontaine, J.S. 1972 [1962] Gisu Marriage and Affinal Relations. In Marriage in Tribal Societies. M. Fortes, ed. Pp. 88-120. Cambridge Papers in Social Anthropology, No. 3. Cambridge: Cambridge University Press.

La Fontaine, J.S. 1979 Land and the Political Community in Bugisu. In Politics in Leadership: A Comparative Perspective. W.A. Shack and P.S. Cohen, eds. Pp. 94–114. Oxford: Clarendon Press.

Turner, V. 1969 Symbolization and Patterning in the Circumcision Rites of Two Bantu-Speaking Societies. In Man in Africa. M. Douglas and P. Kaberry, eds. Pp. 229–244. New York: Tavistock Publications.

Kpelle

Bledsoe, C.H. 1980 Women and Marriage in Kpelle Society. Stanford: Stanford University Press.

Gibbs, J.L. 1963 Marital Instability among the Kpelle: Towards a Theory of Epainogamy. American Anthropologist 65: 552–573.

Gibbs, J.L. 1965 The Kpelle of Liberia. In Peoples of Africa. J.L. Gibbs, ed. Pp. 197–240. New York: Holt, Rinehart and Winston.

Samia (Abaluyia, Abasamia)

Cattell, M. 1989 Old Age in Rural Kenya: Gender, the Life Course and Social Change. Ph.D. Dissertation, Bryn Mawr College.

Cattell, M. 1992 Praise the Lord and Say No to Men: Older Women Empowering Themselves in Samia, Kenya. Journal of Cross-Cultural Gerontology 7: 307–330.

Cattell, M. 1998. "Nowadays It Isn't Easy to Advise": Grandmothers and Granddaughters among Abaluyia of Kenya. In Women among Women: Anthropological Perspectives on Female Age Hierarchies. J. Dickerson-Putman and J.K. Brown, eds. Pp. 30–51. Urbana: University of Illinois Press.

CIRCUM-MEDITERRANEAN

Al Murrah Bedouin

Barfield, T.J. 1993 The Nomadic Alternative. Englewood Cliffs, NJ: Prentice Hall.
Cole, D.P. 1975 Nomads of the Nomads: The Al Murrah Bedonin of the Empty Quarter. Chicago: Aldine.

North Somali Herders

Lewis, I.M. 1962 Marriage and the Family in Northern Somaliland. East African Studies No. 15. Kampala, Uganda: East Africa Institute of Social Research.
Lewis, I.M. 1965 The Northern Pastoral Somali of the Horn. In Peoples of Africa. J.L. Gibbs, ed. Pp. 319–360. New York: Holt, Rinehart and Winston.

North Yemeni Villagers

Dorsky, S. 1986 Women of 'Amran': A Middle Eastern Ethnographic Study. Salt Lake City: University of Utah Press.
Makhlouf, C. 1979 Changing Veils: Women and Modernization in North Yemen. Austin: University of Texas Press.

Portuguese Maritime Villagers

Cole, S. 1991 Women of the Praia: Work and Lives in a Portuguese Coastal Community. Princeton, NJ: Princeton University Press.

Turkish Villagers

Benedict, P. 1976 Aspects of the Domestic Cycle in a Turkish Provincial Town. In Mediterranean Family Structures. J.G. Peristiany, ed. Pp. 219–241, New York: Cambridge University Press.
Delany, C. 1991 The Seed and the Soil: Gender and Cosmology in Turkish Village Society. Berkeley: University of California Press.
Fallers, L. and M.C. Fallers 1976 Sex Roles in Edremit. In Mediterranean Family Structures. J.G. Peristiany, ed. Pp. 243–260. New York: Cambridge University Press.
Kandiyoti, D. 1990 Rural Transformation in Turkey and Its Implications for Women's Status. In Women, Family and Social Change in Turkey. F. Ozbay, ed. Pp. 91–104. Bangkok: UNESCO.
Magnarella, P.J. 1974 Tradition and Change in a Turkish Town. Cambridge, MA: Schenkman.
Makal, M. 1954 A Village in Anatolia. W. Deedes, trans. London: Vallentine, Mitchell.
Morvaridi, B. 1992 Gender Relations in Agriculture: Women in Turkey. Economic Development and Cultural Change. 40(3): 567–586.
Pierce, J.E. 1964 Life in a Turkish Village. New York: Holt, Rinehart and Winston.
Roper, J. 1974 The Women of Nar. London: Faber and Faber.
Stirling, P. 1972 [1965] Turkish Village. London: Weidenfeld and Nicolson.

Toprak, B. 1990 Emancipated but Unliberated Women in Turkey: The Impact of Islam. In Women, Family and Social Change in Turkey. F. Ozbay, ed. Pp. 39–49. Bangkok: UNESCO.

EASTERN EURASIA

Chukchee

Bogoras, W. 1904–9. The Chukchee. American Museum of Natural History, Memoirs. The Jesup North Pacific Expedition (1897–1903). Vol. 11, Nos. 1–3. New York: G.E. Stechert.

Korea

Brandt, V.S.R. 1971 A Korean Village: Between Farm and Sea. Cambridge, MA: Harvard University Press.

Choi, J. 1976 Family System. In Korean Society. Chun Shin-Yong, general ed. Pp. 15–33. Korean Culture Series 6. Seoul, Korea: International Cultural Foundation.

Kendall, L. 1985 Shamans, Housewives, and Other Restless Spirits: Women in Korean Ritual Life. Honolulu: University of Hawaii Press.

Kim, C.S. 1988 Faithful Endurance: An Ethnography of Korean Family Dispersal. Tucson: University of Arizona Press.

Osgood, C. 1951 The Koreans and Their Culture. New York: Ronald Press.

Malaysian Villagers

Raybeck, D. 1979 The Ideal and the Real: The Status of Women in Kelanta Malay Society. Paper delivered at the 19th annual meeting of the Northeastern Anthropological Association, Henniker, NH.

Raybeck, D. 1992 A Diminished Dichotomy: Kelantan Malay and Traditional Chinese Perspectives. In In Her Prime: New Views of Middle-Aged Women. Second edition. V. Kerns and J.K. Brown, eds. Pp. 173–189. Urbana: University of Illinois Press.

Strange, H. 1981 Rural Malay Women in Tradition and Transition. New York: Praeger.

Wilson, P.J. 1967 A Malay Village and Malaysia: Social Values and Rural Development. New Haven, CT: Human Relations Area Files Press.

Marri Baluch

Pehrson, R. 1966 The Social Organization of the Marri Baluch. Fredrik Barth, comp. Viking Fund Publications in Anthropology No. 43. New York: Wenner-Gren Foundation for Anthropological Research.

Rajputs

Hitchcock, J. and L. Minturn 1963 The Rajputs of Khalapur, India. In Six Cultures: Studies of Child Rearing. B. Whiting, ed. Pp. 207–361. New York: John Wiley and Sons.

Jacobson, D. 1977 The Women of North and Central India: Goddesses and Wives. In Women in India: Two Perspectives. D. Jacobson and S.S. Wadley, eds. Pp. 17–111. New Delhi: South Asia Books.

Mandelbaum, D. 1970 Society in India. Vol. 1, Continuity and Change. Berkeley: University of California Press.

Mandelbaum, D. 1988 Women's Seclusion and Men's Honor: Sex Roles in North India, Bangladesh, and Pakistan. Tucson: University of Arizona Press.

Minturn, L. 1993 Sita's Daughters: Coming Out of Purdah: The Rajput Women of Khalapur Revisited. New York: Oxford Press.

Minturn, L. and J. Hitchcock 1966 The Rajputs of Khalapur, India. New York: John Wiley.

ISLAND PACIFIC

Bontoc Igorot

Jenks, A.E. 1905 The Bontoc Igorot. Ethnological Survey, Vol. 1. Manila: Bureau of Public Printing.

Iban

Davison, J. and V. Sutlive 1991 The Children of *Nising:* Images of Headhunting and Male Sexuality in Iban Ritual and Oral literature. In Female and Male in Borneo: Contributions and Challenges to Gender Studies. V.H. Sutlive, ed. Pp. 153–230. Monograph Series, Vol. 1. Williamsburg, VA: Borneo Research Council.

Drake, R.A. 1991 The Cultural Logic of Textile Weaving Practices among the Ibanic People. In Female and Male in Borneo: Contributions and Challenges to Gender Studies. V.H. Sutlive, ed. Pp. 271–293. Monograph Series, Vol. 1. Williamsburg, VA: Borneo Research Council.

Kedit, P.M. 1991 "Meanwhile, Back Home . . .": *Bejalai* and Their Effects on Iban Men and Women. In Female and Male in Borneo: Contributions and Challenges to Gender Studies. V.H. Sutlive, ed. Pp. 295–316. Monograph Series, Vol. 1. Williamsburg, VA: Borneo Research Council.

Mashman, V. 1991 Warriors and Weavers: A Study of Gender Relations among the Iban of Sarawak. In Female and Male in Borneo: Contributions and Challenges to Gender Studies. V.H. Sutlive, ed. Pp. 231–270. Monograph Series, Vol. 1. Williamsburg, VA: Borneo Research Council.

Sutlive, V.H. 1978 The Iban of Sarawak. Arlington Heights, IL: AHM Publishing Corp.

Sutlive, V.H., ed. 1991 Female and Male in Borneo: Contributions and Challenges to Gender Studies. Monograph Series, Vol 1. Williamsburg, VA: Borneo Research Council.

Maori

Buck, P. (Te Rangi Hiroa) 1949 The Coming of the Maori. Wellington, New Zealand: Whitcombe and Tombs.

Firth, R. 1929 Primitive Economy of the New Zealand Maori. New York: E.P. Dutton.

Hanson, F.A. 1982 Female Pollution in Polynesia? Journal of the Polynesian Society 91: 335–381.

Metge, A.J. 1967 The Maoris of New Zealand. New York: Humanities Press.

Sinclair, K.P. 1985 Koro and Kuia: Aging and Gender among the Maori of New Zealand. In Aging and Its Transformations. D.A. Counts and D.R. Counts, eds. Pp. 27–46. ASAO Monograph No. 10. New York: Academic Press.

Sinclair, K.P. 1992 A Study in Pride and Prejudice: Maori Women at Midlife. In In Her Prime: New Views of Middle-Aged Women. V. Kerns and J.K. Brown, eds. Second edition. Pp. 113–137. Urbana: University of Illinois Press.

Nagovisi

Mitchell, D.D., II 1971 Gardening for Money: Land and Agriculture in Nagovisi. Ph.D. Dissertation, Harvard University.

Mitchell, D.D., II 1976 Land and Agriculture in Nagovisi, Papua New Guinea. Monograph 3. Boroko, Papua New Guinea: Institute of Applied Social and Economic Research.

Nash, J. 1974 Matriliny and Modernization: The Nagovisi of South Bougainville. New Guinea Research Bulletin No. 55. Port Morseby: New Guinea Research Unit, Australian National University.

Nash, J. 1978 A Note on Groom Price. American Anthropologist 80: 106–108.

Nash, J. 1981 Sex, Money, and the Status of Women in Aboriginal South Bougainville. American Ethnologist 8(1): 107–126.

Nash, J. 1984 Women, Work, and Change in Nagovisi. In Rethinking Women's Roles: Perspectives from the Pacific. D. O'Brien and S.W. Tiffany, eds. Pp. 94–119. Berkeley: University of California Press.

Nash, J. 1990 [1987] Gender Attributes and Inequality: Men's Strength and Women's Talk among the Nagovisi. In Dealing with Inequality: Analysing Gender Relations in Melanesia and Beyond. M.Strathern, ed. Pp. 150–173. New York: Cambridge University Press.

Nash, J. 1992 Factors Relating to Infrequent Domestic Violence among the Nagovisi. In Sanctions and Sanctuary: Cultural Perspectives on the Beating of Wives. D.A. Counts, J.K. Brown, and J.C. Campbell, eds. Pp. 99–110. Boulder: Westview Press. Also in Pacific Studies 13(3): 127–140.

Samoa

Holmes, L.D. 1974 Samoan Village. New York: Holt, Rinehart and Winston.
Holmes, L.D. and E.R. Holmes 1992 Samoan Village: Then and Now. Fort Worth: Harcourt.
Tuiteleleapaga, N. 1980 Samoa, Yesterday, Today and Tomorrow. Great Neck, NY: Todd and Honeywell.

NORTH AMERICA

Havasupai

Dobyns, H.F. and R.C. Euler 1974 [1960] Socio-Political Structure and Ethnic Group Concept of the Pai of Northwestern Arizona. In Havasupai Indians. R. Manners, H. Dobyns, and R. Euler, eds. Pp. 177–274. New York: Garland.
Smithson, C.L. 1959 The Havasupai Woman. Anthropological Papers of the University of Utah Department of Anthropology No. 38. HRAF file NT 14.

Kaska

Honigmann, J.J. 1964 [1954] The Kaska Indians: An Ethnographic Reconstruction. Reprinted edition. Yale University Publications in Anthropology No. 51. New Haven, CT: Human Relations Area Files Press.

Ojibwa

Landes, R. 1938 The Ojibwa Woman. New York: Columbia University Press.
Landes, R. 1969 [1937] Ojibwa Sociology. New York: AMS Press.

Papago

Underhill, R.M. 1939 Social Organization of the Papago Indians. Columbia University Contributions to Anthropology, Vol. 30. New York: Columbia University Press.
Underhill, R. 1979 Papago Woman. New York: Holt, Rinehart and Winston.

Tlingit

Emmons, G.T. 1991 The Tlingit Indians. F. de Laguna, ed. Seattle: University of Washington Press.
Gunther, E. 1972 Indian Life on the Northwest Coast of North America. Chicago: University of Chicago Press.
Jones, L.F. 1970 [1914] A Study of the Thlingets of Alaska. New York: Johnson Reprint Co.
Krause, A. 1956 [1883?] The Tlingit Indians: Results of a Trip to the Northwest Coast of America and the Bering Sea. E. Gunther, trans. Seattle: University of Washington Press.

Oberg, K. 1966 Crime and Punishment in Tlingit Society. In Indians of the North Pacific Coast. T. McFeat, ed. Pp. 209–222. Seattle: University of Washington Press.

Oberg, K. 1973 The Social Economy of the Tlingit Indians. Seattle: University of Washington Press.

SOUTH AMERICA

Maroni River Carib

Kloos, P. 1969 Female Initiation among the Maroni River Caribs. American Anthropologist 71: 898-905.

Kloos, P. 1971 The Maroni River Caribs of Surinam. Assen, The Netherlands: Van Gorcum.

Quechua (Inca)

Allen, C.J. 1981 To Be Quechua: The Symbolism of Coca Chewing in Highland Peru. American Ethnologist 8(1): 157–171.

Allen, C.J. 1988 The Hold Life Has: Coca and Cultural Identity in an Andean Community. Washington, DC: Smithsonian Institution Press.

Steward, J. and L.C. Faron 1959 Native Peoples of South America. New York: McGraw-Hill.

Webster, S.S. 1977 Kinship and Affinity in a Native Quechua Community. In Andean Kinship and Marriage. R. Bolton and E. Meyer, eds. Pp. 28-42. Special Publication of the American Anthropology Association, No. 7. Washington, DC: American Anthropology Association.

Siriono

Holmberg, A. 1969 [1950] Nomads of the Long Bow. Prospect Heights, IL: Waveland Press.

Yagua

Fejos, P. 1943 Ethnography of the Yagua. Viking Fund Publications in Anthropology, No. 1. New York: Wenner-Gren Foundation for Anthropological Research.

Steward, J.H. and A. Metraux 1946–59 The Peban Tribes. In Handbook of South American Indians, Vol. 3. J. Steward, ed. Pp. 727–748. Washington, DC: U.S. Government Printing Office.

Zinacantan (Maya)

Collier, J.F. 1974 Women in Politics. In Women, Culture, and Society. M. Rosaldo and L. Lamphere, eds. Pp. 89–97. Stanford: Stanford University Press.

Devereaux, L. 1990 [1987] Gender Differences and the Relations of Inequality in Zinacantan. In Dealing with Inequality: Analysing Gender Relations in

Melanesia and Beyond. M. Strathern, ed. Pp. 89–111. New York: Cambridge University Press.

Haviland, L.K.M. 1978 The Social Relations of Work in a Peasant Community. Ph.D. Dissertation, Harvard University.

Haviland, L.K. and J.B. Haviland 1982 "Inside the Fence": The Social Basis of Privacy in Nabenchauk. Estudios de Cultura Maya 14: 323–351.

Vogt, E.Z. 1969 Zinacantan: A Maya Community in the Highlands of Chiapas. Cambridge, MA: Belknap Press.

CONTRIBUTORS

JUDITH K. BROWN is a professor of anthropology at Oakland University in Rochester, Michigan. She is the coeditor of *In Her Prime: New Views of Middle-Aged Women* (1992, with Virginia Kerns) and *Sanctions and Sanctuary: Cultural Perspectives on the Beating of Wives* (1992, with Dorothy Counts and Jacquelyn Campbell).

VICTORIA K. BURBANK is an associate professor of anthropology at the University of Western Australia. Her publications on women's lives in Aboriginal Australia include *Aboriginal Adolescence* (1988) and *Fighting Women* (1994).

MARIA G. CATTELL teaches at Millersville University and is a research associate at the Field Museum of Natural History. A former contributing editor to the *Anthropology Newsletter,* she is the author of a number of articles and book chapters and is coauthor of *Old Age in Global Perspective: Cross-Cultural and Cross-National Views* (1994, with Albert Cattell). She is the president of the Association for Anthropology and Gerontology.

NANCY FONER is a professor of anthropology at the State University of New York, Purchase. She has written two books on aging: *Ages in Conflict: A Cross Cultural Perspective on Inequality between Old and Young* (1984) and *The Caregiving Dilemma: Work in an American Nursing Home* (1994). She has also published several books and many articles on social change in rural Jamaica and Jamaican migrants in London and New York.

JEANETTE DICKERSON-PUTMAN is an associate professor and chair of the Department of Anthropology at Indiana University–Indianapolis. Her research and publications focus on age, gender, and the development process; the religious economy; the gendered life course; caregivers to the elderly; and oceania cultures.

RITA S. GALLIN is a professor of sociology at Michigan State University. Her research focuses on Taiwan, where she has carried out seven field studies on gender and socioeconomic change in one rural community. She has published numerous articles and book chapters on this work, edited five volumes on women and global transformation, and is the founding editor of Westview Press's annual *Women and International Development.*

SUSAN M. KENYON is an associate professor and director of anthropology at Butler University, Indianapolis. She has carried out field research among the West Coast

Indians of Vancouver Island (the "Nootka"), in a West Javanese *kampung* of Indonesia, and in Central Sudan. Her publications include *The Kyuquot Way* (1981) and *Five Women of Sennar* (1991); she is also the editor of *The Sudanese Woman* (1987).

WINIFRED L. MITCHELL teaches anthropology at Minnesota's Mankato State University, where she chairs the department. Her field research has been in the Peruvian Andes and the Bolivian lowlands with peasant populations, and she has published several articles on Andean women's power. She recently served as the column editor of the Association for Feminist Anthropology in the *Anthropology Newsletter.*

MARY S. McDONALD PAVELKA is an associate professor of anthropology at the University of Calgary and the author of *Monkeys of the Mesquite: The Social Life of the South Texas Snow Monkey* (1993). Her doctoral research focused on the social manifestations of aging in female Japanese monkeys, and she continues to publish on the topics of aging, menopause, and the evolution of human sexuality.

DENISE PILATO, who teaches in the science and technology program at the College of Lyman Briggs at Michigan State University and in the American studies program at Central Michigan University, will receive a Ph.D. in American studies from Michigan State University in 1998. Her research focuses on gender and technology in American culture, with an emphasis on women inventors of the nineteenth century.

THERESE SARAH is a senior associate at the Mid-continent Regional Educational Laboratory in Aurora, Colorado.

PERLA SUBBAIAH is a professor of statistics in the Department of Mathematical Sciences at Oakland University in Rochester, Michigan. He has published statistical works and cross-disciplinary research, particularly in medicine and science.

INDEX

A000017018074